HIDDEN
LANCASHIRE

Ron Freethy

HIDDEN
LANCASHIRE
Ron Freethy

To Pat
with best wishes
Ron Freethy

COUNTRYSIDE BOOKS
NEWBURY, BERKSHIRE

COUNTRYSIDE BOOKS
3 Catherine Road
Newbury, Berkshire

ISBN 1 85306 420 3

Front cover photograph of the packhorse bridge at Wycoller by
Bill Meadows
Back cover photograph taken at Much Hoole church by the
author
Line illustrations by Mavis Stewart

Designed by Graham Whiteman
Produced through MRM Associates Ltd., Reading
Printed by Woolnough Bookbinding, Irthlingborough

INTRODUCTION

Lancashire is one of those counties which has a long and fascinating history, but many of its architectural gems were swamped by the sprawl of the Industrial Revolution.

Until as late as the 1980s the grime of industry was accepted and both visitors and locals seemed happy to seek out the areas of unspoiled countryside. Gradually however, as the cotton and coal industries have declined, with associated improvement in pollution levels, the remaining pieces of ancient history are slowly being rediscovered. This has made the writing of this book particularly enjoyable as fascinating places are continually being rediscovered.

The incentive to discover the hidden aspects of the old county of Lancashire was due in the main to three local radio stations and three newspapers. Listeners to BBC Radio Merseyside, GMR Talk and BBC Radio Lancashire and readers of the *Bolton Evening News*, *Blackpool Evening Gazette* and especially the *Lancashire Evening Telegraph*, all seemed to be fascinated by tales of the forgotten bits of the county and invariably added their own memories to the programmes and articles.

Thanks are due to Sally Wheatman of GMR Talk, Manchester; Evelyn Draper and Andy Tennant of BBC Radio Merseyside; and Alison Brown of BBC Radio Lancashire. Three newspaper editors have also shown great enthusiasm for this project and mention must be made of Richard Catlow of Blackpool's *Evening Gazette* and now the *Rochdale Observer*; Andrew Smith and Derek Grocock of the *Bolton Evening News*; and Peter Butterfield of the *Lancashire Evening Telegraph*. A number of programmes for Granada Television which were co-presented by Bob Smithies also focussed on hidden aspects of Lancashire's past.

All these people have played their part but special thanks must go to Marlene Freethy, who contributed much of the research concerning all these projects and who also prepared the typescript and did the picture research for the illustrations. Helpful comments during the editing process were given by the editorial staff of Countryside Books.

Ron Freethy
Peel, Nr. Blackpool

Hidden
LANCASHIRE

LANCASTER

BLACKPOOL

PRESTON

BURNLEY

BLACKBURN

Southport

Chorley

Ormskirk

Skelmersdale

ABBEYSTEAD

Wyresdale is one of the unsung valleys of England but so beautiful that it is difficult to understand why this should be so. The river Wyre has two sources, each rising on the mossy slopes of the Trough of Bowland. These are the Tarnbrook and the Marshaw Wyre, and they meet near Abbeystead, at a lonely spot called Emmott. The name of the first substantial settlement indicates that at one time monks were settled at their Abbey Stead. A group of 12th-century Cistercians made an attempt to establish an abbey but apparently found the climate too tough – there are often very heavy snowfalls in early winter and late spring – and so they moved to Ireland.

A pleasant walk of about a mile from Abbeystead, along a tree fringed road, leads to the remote Christ's Church-over-Wyresdale. This gets its local name of the Shepherds' church from an inscription above the door, which reads 'O-Ye Shepherds hear the word of the Lord'. The stained glass windows depict scenes from the Bible associated with sheep. Within the porch is a narrow beam on which the shepherds could hang their crooks and in the vestry is a collection of old instruments, many crude, locally made and used to accompany the services before an organ was installed.

Such a vast catchment area was obviously too valuable to be ignored by planners during the periods of industrial expansion and water has been piped to the northern towns for nearly 100 years. An explosion occurred and caused grievous loss of life among a group of tourists inside the Abbeystead pumping station in the spring of 1984. An official enquiry suggested that vegetation had become trapped in the filter system; when this rotted, methane gas was produced. The explosion occurred when someone lit a cigarette. A memorial plaque has been erected close to the site.

AFFETSIDE

Situated on the moors between the modern towns of Burnley and Bolton and on part of the Romans' Watling Street, Affetside is well signed off the A676. The village has a claim to be Lancashire's own version of Golgotha – here is an historic

Saxon preaching cross and a place of the skull.

At one time Affetside was important because it stood on the coach road and at the half-way point between London and Edinburgh. An attractive cross on the main street records this fact and it is very well cared for, with a seat provided for those who have arrived on foot and feel like a rest.

It is far better, however, to have a drink at the Packhorse Inn. This hostelry indicates that Affetside was an important place on the rough tracks prior to the turnpike age. When ordering your drink look up to the shelf above the optics. This pub obviously serves more than one type of spirit, as a skull sits comfortably on a shelf.

The skull is that of George Whewell who performed the gruesome task of executing Lord Derby (see also *Bolton*). A local farmer, Whewell was seemingly so unpopular that he had been buried in unconsecrated ground. The skull has been moved from its position several times but this has always been followed by 'strange happenings' and very soon replaced.

Anyone on the lookout for the secret places of Lancashire should walk or drive slowly up Watling Street into Affetside, enter the Packhorse and have the 'spirit' to make eye to eye socket contact with Lord Derby's executioner.

ALTHAM

Now dominated by a modern complex of factories producing electrical components, the hamlet of Altham still looks pretty and stands on the fertile banks of the river Calder. Its large cemetery is sliced in two by the busy modern road between Burnley and Blackburn. The lovely old church contains a gem – a font donated by Abbot John Paslew, the last abbot of Whalley. It is beautifully and ornately carved and depicts the tools associated with the crucifixion including a hammer and vicious looking nails.

The east window is also of interest although few people these days realise its significance. It shows colourful scenes from the life of Christ and also celebrates the life of James Hacking. Even students of the early cotton industry ask who was James Hacking? He invented a carding machine which accelerated the preparation of yarn prior to it being worked on the loom by combing the cotton fibres straight. This saved

Altham churchyard.

local mill owners a great deal of money and there is no doubt that Hacking deserves his memorial. He may have preferred the industrialists to part with more of their brass while he was alive – some hope!

In the church there is a memorial mourning the loss of 68 men and boys killed on 7th November 1883 by an explosion caused by 'damp gas' at the nearby Moorfield Colliery. All trace of these mines has now vanished.

ANGLEZARKE

Anglezarke is reached via Belmont and from the A674 Blackburn to Chorley road. It has long been one of the least explored areas of Lancashire.

During the 1980s a footpath was laid out following the route of the old lead mine workings which were in operation from 1692 to around 1840. In the 1930s, during the worst depression of the century, work was found for the local unemployed filling in the dangerous lead mine shafts (going down) and adits (running horizontally).

High on the moor is an almost unknown but very attractive memorial erected in memory of the crew of a Wellington bomber killed when the aircraft crashed on the spot in 1943. From the memorial there are views across the valley to Winter Hill with its television transmitter mast dominating the horizon. It carries navigational lights which ensure that modern aircraft en route for Manchester Airport have a much safer passage than the unfortunate Wellington.

ASHURST BEACON

—— Straddling a ridge overlooking the fertile south Lancashire plain above Parbold, the 304 acre Beacon Country Park is patchworked by belts of oak and newly planted conifers. The park is now better known than Ashurst Beacon which stands proudly on the summit. Though prominent, the beacon, once on private ground, stands on the opposite side of the road to the country park, perhaps leading visitors to think that the nearby inn of the same name is actually on the site of the original beacon.

The walk to the beacon is not too steep and is well worth the effort. The path is lined with gorse which provides ideal habitat for breeding stonechat and whinchat. The beacon formed part of an ancient chain of warning fires which stretched from Everton Brow above Liverpool to Lancaster Castle. This chain was vital during the period when the Spanish Armada was threatening, although thankfully they never had to be torched.

The word beacon is self-explanatory but who was Ashurst? Some confusion arises because Sir William Ashurst only came into the picture when Napoleon was threatening to invade England. Sir William lived down the hill in the 16th-century Ashurst Hall near the village of Dalton. In front of the house is a magnificently fortified gatehouse which may well be 14th century in origin.

Sir William Ashurst decided in 1797 that a huge and more permanent beacon should be constructed to help meet and overcome the mighty threat posed by Napoleon's army. The beacon was provided with a cast iron fire box and holes in its chimney-like walls have now unfortunately been filled in. These provided 'windows' out of which the flames could belch their warning and essential air could reach them. The beacon was in a sad state of repair by 1940 and would have collapsed had not remedial measures been taken.

The Beacon is still a fine though little known monument from which can be seen the Lakeland hills, Blackpool Tower, the Welsh mountains, the Pennines and the Peak District of Derbyshire.

ATHERTON

—— Here is one of the most remarkable chapels to be found anywhere in Britain – built by a non-conformist minister using a pension given to him by a grateful king.

When the Act of Uniformity was passed young James Woods of Atherton refused to conform but he was in dispute with church doctrine, not directly with the king himself.

When the Scots, supporting Charles Stewart, the Young Pretender, came rampaging through Lancashire the last person George I could have expected to fight for him would have been this particular church minister. The cleric and his family, however, raised 80 armed men and these were largely instrumental in preventing the Scots crossing the bridge over the river Ribble at Walton-le-Dale. The pension granted by the grateful monarch was partly used to build Chowbent chapel at Atherton in 1721.

The interior of the chapel is impressive to say the least with box pews and panelled galleries reached via a graceful staircase.

AUGHTON

—— A narrow road lined by the Liverpool strawberry and potato fields, made famous by the songs of the Beatles, leads to this still surprisingly attractive village dominated by the magnificent spire of St Michael's church. Its rectors are listed from 1246 onwards. Much of the church's splendid medieval architecture remains, although some extensive and rather brutal restoration was carried out in 1914. In the bell tower are 14th-century wooden figures depicting the Stanleys, whose founder, Sir John Stanley (1350-1414), became Lord Derby and ruler of the Isle of Man; the three legs of Man are clearly shown on the carved heraldic shields carried by the figures. In the churchyard is a sundial of 1736 which is inscribed 'I only count the sunny hours'.

Opposite the church and close to the Stanley Arms is Aughton Old Hall, not open to the public but easily visible from the road. There are the remains of a 15th-century pele tower in the front garden.

Aughton is largely ignored these days because most tourists mistakenly feel that the Liverpool area has nothing of interest to offer. This is another example of Lancashire's fair face being almost swamped by urban sprawl.

BACUP

High on the breezy hills above Bacup rises the infant river Irwell which once powered the town's mighty cotton mills, now alas all silent. The museum of the Bacup Naturalists known as the 'Nats', founded in 1878 as an artisans' naturalists' society by cotton operatives (one of many such societies in the north), displays a spectacular jumble of exhibits recalling the mid-19th century heyday of cotton and coal, clog and shawl, trap and tram. The richness of local wildlife is reflected in exhibitions of birds and butterflies, moths, mayflies and mammals. Known to surprisingly few people this museum is a treasure house of local history and natural history.

The museum building on Yorkshire Street, which also belongs to the Society, was once a public house and had served its time as a doss house. In an outhouse an old power loom has been restored and is now in ear-splitting working order.

In the small garden protected by a wall is a collection of old street signs. I have often sat in this garden listening to old folk with young memories describing what life was like in boomtime Bacup when these signs were needed for directions and not confined to a garden.

The museum is still run by committee members with no formal academic training. This unfortunately prevents some who should know better from treating the place as a serious museum. A treasure trove such as this should receive the attention it so richly deserves.

BARROW BRIDGE

The nearby town of Bolton, close enough to Barrow Bridge to walk, was once a village surrounded by magnificent upland scenery, and aptly named Bolton-in-the-Moors. The change from small village to large town came about through cotton replacing wool and inventors such as Samuel Crompton, altering the base of industry from village cottage to town mill.

The intermediate period between village and town is clearly seen at Barrow Bridge, recognised by those who live there as a time-encapsulated reminder of the early Industrial Revolution. It is reached by turning off the A58 at Moss Bank Way near Halliwell.

Port Sunlight on Merseyside and Saltaire near Bradford are well known and much publicised model villages built by enlightened industrialists for their workers. Barrow Bridge is one of the less well known villages and unique in the sense that it is said to be the first workers' co-operative ever set up in England (see also *Rochdale*).

There had been a small textile mill on this site for some time when, in 1830, the complex was bought by Robert Gardner of Manchester who appointed a very able mill manager named Thomas Bailey. The partnership worked so well that profits soared and new mills were built.

The management looked after their workforce and provided them with pleasant houses each with its own garden. Compared with the conditions in which town based mill workers lived this was sheer luxury. The children of Robert Gardner's workers were provided with a splendid school and there was also a lecture hall and a village institute.

In 1851 Prince Albert and Benjamin Disraeli visited Barrow Bridge which was then regarded as a wonder of its age. Later General Booth, the founder of the Salvation Army, tried to buy the village and use it as a base from which to launch his 'war on poverty'. Alas the General failed to meet the asking price and the deal fell through.

Although the mills have been demolished, the houses with their colourful gardens remain overlooking the stream which once powered the early mills. Some of the houses look magnificent with their walls covered by a deep red tangle of Virginia creeper.

Near the bridge is a weir built to accelerate the stream prior to its reaching the mill wheels. This now safe area is very popular with children who love fishing and dogs which enjoy splashing about in the shallow water. From the bridge a set of steep steps climb through woodland and up onto the moors. The colours and scenery are so attractive here that it is hard to believe that Barrow Bridge is secreted away in a hollow close to the centre of Bolton and not in the heart of the Lake District or the Yorkshire Dales.

BARROWFORD

It is amazing how often history lurks among an industrial sprawl. Set just off the M65, Barrowford, between Nelson and Colne, looks to be a boring ribbon of a village through which traffic slowly winds its way. Those who fail to stop don't know what they are missing – here are some wonderful and historic buildings, the haunt of Thimblethung Thistlethwaite and one of the most attractive and largest packhorse bridges in England.

Set back from the main road is a building, now known as the Lamb Working Men's Club, dating to 1626 and beautifully restored. The Lamb has a typical tongue in cheek Lancashire tale to tell. On May Day during Victorian times the building was the starting point for a walk up to nearby Pendle Hill organised by American Tom, who wished to celebrate a return to his native haunts after a spell in the States. His followers first had to eat a pudding made from nettles, eggs, dripping and meat but nobody was allowed to drink alcohol until they had recited the following rhyme without any hesitation: 'Thimblethung Thistlethwaite who thinking to thrive through thick and thin, through throwing three thimbles hither and thither, and was thwarted and thwacked by thirty three thousand thick thorns.' You would have to be sober to cope with that.

None of Barrowford's buildings get the recognition they

deserve, but even the few visitors who do appreciate their worth usually miss the most remarkable structure in the village.

Following American Tom's route along the Gisburn road and upstream on the banks of Pendle Water, and then turning left at the next modern bridge leads to Higherford bridge. Although known locally as the Roman bridge, it is actually medieval in origin. The bridge is surrounded by trees whose leaves obscure the view in summer but enough can always be seen to reveal that it is in a splendid state of repair. John Wesley preached from the summit of the hump of the single spanned bridge at the time when Barrowford was having to make its choice between history and industry. Industry won, and as the bridge became too narrow for busy traffic it was totally neglected. Now history is fighting back as is proved to those willing to search out this splendid bridge.

BARTON

Many have heard or read about the engineering wonders of the Barton Aqueduct but few have seen it. The aqueduct is unusual in that it carries one canal (the Bridgewater) over another (the Manchester Ship). It has, however, other unique features. Very skilful engineering means that the section immediately above the Ship Canal can be swung aside to allow ocean-going ships to pass through.

The moveable section is a 330 ft long steel cylinder swinging on a central pivot. When operating the Bridgewater section has huge rubber-lined wedges which push together to form watertight joints. In the days of horse drawn traffic a towpath was provided to enable two animals to pass without their ropes becoming entangled.

There has been an aqueduct at Barton since 1770 when James Brindley had to carry his canal over the river Irwell. When this section of the Irwell was incorporated into the Ship Canal in 1893 Brindley's aqueduct, a masterpiece in its own right, was replaced by the present bridge.

During the excavations to construct the swing aqueduct in 1890 a fine example of a prehistoric dug-out canoe was unearthed from the heavy clay soil.

BASHALL

Bashall Town is not a town these days but a hamlet consisting of just a few scattered dwellings. The nearby Bashall Eaves, scene of the unsolved Red Pump Inn murder of 1936, is a pleasant spot built around a small green. The old village pump stands outside the pub and gleams as scarlet as a post box. What has this small village within range of Clitheroe and Whalley got to offer the visitor? The area is steeped in history, teems with natural history and has retained all of its old country charm.

The region was governed by the Talbots who lived at Bashall Hall which, thankfully, is still in private hands and has been lovingly restored. It can easily be seen across rolling fields from the road leading from Bashall Eaves to Waddington. The Tudor Bashall Hall receives little attention despite its architectural interest and the fact that it has a unique feature. This is the retainers' dwelling at the rear which in some ways is more interesting and actually older than the hall itself and is a fine example of the accommodation which the gentry had to provide for their own private armies during the Wars of the Roses, which raged from 1455 to 1485. The Talbot and the Tempest families were at each others' throats and their soldiers had to be kept fit and well housed. Conditions must have been reminiscent of the modern day feuds of the Italian Mafia families. The old retainers' stables and the soldiers' sleeping quarters are still in good repair despite being used as farm outbuildings during the early years of this century.

BILSBORROW

Bilsborrow is situated along the A6 road near Garstang, and on a bridge over the Lancaster Canal Owd Nell's is described as a thatched hamlet.

There seems to be thatch everywhere, and the whole area is like a journey backwards in time. Close to the canal are an old schoolhouse, a bargees' shop, gift shop and a saddlers' shop set among the entrances to Owd Nell's Pub and Guy's Lodgings which is an up-market restaurant and motel. On the walls of several buildings are a number of tin advertising boards including those for Black Cat cigarettes, Rajah cigars, Birds custard powder sold in tin boxes, and the days are recalled when a delivery van cost less than £200. And what about Elliman's Rub which smelled like a rugby dressing room and made sprains feel as if they had to be set on fire before a cure was possible? All this is exciting enough but some weekends are made even more enjoyable by a jazz band playing in the open square.

Canal craft of all shapes and sizes are moored along the canal corridor and their colours always add to the beauty of the scene. The life of a bargee in the days when essential goods were carried between Kendal and Preston was tough especially at the times of loading and unloading, but the journey itself was both lock free and passed through idyllic countryside. They were proud of their floating homes and even their household utensils were colourfully decorated. Such items can now be bought from the bargees' shop. The whole complex is a reminder of the days when much of Lancashire's history was carried upon a cut of water.

BLACKO

——— Blacko on a good day can be as beautiful as any 'chocolate box' Cotswold village. This is despite its steep ribbon of a main street which carries a heavy load of traffic.

The Pendle Way crosses the main road just beyond and close to the Moorcock Inn from which a concessionary footpath leads up to Blacko Tower. This is not, as some folk have suggested the Malkin Tower mentioned in the graphic accounts of the Pendle Witches, but was a wild and extravagant gesture by a Yorkshire born grocer who had made his brass in Lancashire. For a number of years I was in correspondence with his family and John Stansfield seems to have been a lovable eccentric.

In 1890 he decided that Blacko at 1,018 feet was not quite high enough to enable him to see into Yorkshire. Until the boundary changes of 1974 Gisburn was in Yorkshire with the old division being between that pleasant village and Blacko. Stansfield therefore built the tower but either his enthusiasm or his brass ran out and the tower was still too low. Yet another folly was thus added to North Country folklore.

How many visitors have rattled along aboard a Blackpool tram which runs along the promenade on its way to Fleetwood – a distance of about seven miles – and alighted at Uncle Tom's Cabin only to wonder where and what it is? Or rather what it was? These days Uncle Tom's Cabin is a modern pub, like one of a thousand others throughout Britain, but why the name?

Up until 1901 Uncle Tom's Cabin was known to most of Lancashire's population. In the mid-19th century Tom Parkinson, who was affectionately known as Uncle Tom had a little wooden hut on the seafront from which he sold non-alcoholic drinks and sweetmeats. He did so well that a shrewd businessman named Taylor, well used to high finance, launched a take over-bid which Uncle Tom could not refuse – he accepted a fiver! In the 1850s business began to boom as the railway reached Blackpool and Mother Nature also played her part. The tide washed up the figurehead of a vessel which had been wrecked in Morecambe Bay. This was the bust of a black man and the event coincided with the popularity of Mrs Beecher Stowe's novel *Uncle Tom's Cabin*. Uncle Tom's was now well and truly on the map and the wooden hut was expanded time and again, dance floors were laid, the best musicians employed and the money rolled in.

Good times never seem to last for ever and two events brought disaster to Uncle Tom's, one man-made the other natural but even more ruthless.

The opening of the Winter Gardens in 1878, which boasted stone elegance and a carpet costing £100, drew the young dancers away from less attractive wooden huts, but their elders who had done their courting under the watchful eye of Uncle Tom remained faithful.

It was the sea, however, which had the last word – it literally cut the ground from beneath Uncle Tom's feet as yard after yard of vulnerable sandy cliff was battered down. Ten yards went in the 1890s and the final blow came in 1901. In June of that year there was a heavy landslip which made it dangerous and under the tearful eyes of hundreds of its ex-customers Uncle Tom's Cabin was demolished.

Now all that remains of this once-popular venue is its name – commemorated by a modern public house.

BLACKSTONE EDGE

This magnificent stretch of Roman road has been preserved, has achieved great fame among historians, and yet is neglected by the public because of the effort to reach it. Good map reading skills and a healthy pair of lungs are essential if Blackstone Edge, which is a 1,475 ft ridge of millstone grit, is to be fully explored. Almost at the summit is a medieval wayside cross called the Aiggin stone which proves that the route was used long after the Romans departed. Indeed parts were turnpiked during the late-18th century but thankfully not all.

Here is the only unaltered section of the road which linked York (Eboracum) and Manchester (Mancunium). It survived here in the high Pennines and crosses the peaty moorlands near the junction of the present road from Rochdale to Halifax. There is a magnificent stretch of about two miles which rejoins the A68 road quite close to Ripponden. Nearby is Baitings reservoir.

Contrary to local superstition the clapper bridge in the area is not Roman – indeed it is modern, having been constructed just to provide work for unemployed men during the depression of the early 1930s. This road, however, has no need of modern additions – it is a world famous monument almost lost in the low clouds of the high Lancashire Pennines.

All the typical features of Roman road construction are here plus one feature which adds a touch of controversy both academic historians and the hunters of hidden Lancashire thrive upon.

Roman roads typically have a raised central section called the Agger from which the cobbled road slopes down to a ditch on either side. The engineering here is of a particularly high standard and the route was probably built around AD 125 when Hadrian's aggressive expansionist policies meant large scale troop movements.

Running down the centre of the road is a prominent groove which some, but by no means all, historians think was worn by the brakes of Roman carriages and chariots. An eminent historian of Roman Britain told me that he was 'worried' by not understanding this structure, but some room for speculation is always healthy and gives incentive to those who enjoy trying to work things out for themselves.

BLEASDALE

Everyone has heard of Stonehenge, almost everybody knows about Avebury but who knows of Lancashire's Timber Circle at Bleasdale? Very few Lancastrians and almost nobody else.

Sheltered by the bulk of the 1,675 ft Fair Snape Fell is the hamlet of Bleasdale, a quiet little spot less than 12 miles from Preston and reached by turning off the A6 Lancaster road at Bilsborrow.

The timber circle does not give up its secrets easily and is reached after a walk of about a mile along a track to Fairsnape farm, starting from a point close to Bleasdale church. This is dedicated to St Eadmer, also known as Eadbert and is the only church in England to be dedicated to a man who took over the work of St Cuthbert at Lindisfarne. Eadmer is buried in the tomb intended for the saint, whose remains now rest in Durham Cathedral.

Though the Victorians knew of it, the site was first discovered in 1898, and the henge has been dated to the Bronze Age at around 800 BC. Originally there were two circles one inside the other with the larger composed of a palisade of huge oak posts. This had a diameter of around 150 ft and was surrounded by a ditch. The overall structure has proved difficult to trace with any accuracy but the second ditch situated between the circles is much clearer. Inside the inner circle was a substantial burial mound found to contain two urns and inside these were calcified bones. This was probably the grave of an important chieftain and his family.

At the time of the discovery none of the actual timbers could be seen above ground. Below ground, however, these were well preserved in the clay soil. Unfortunately the chance was missed to provide Lancashire with a tourist attraction not quite on the scale of Stonehenge, but an impressive one nevertheless. However, the tree stumps were carelessly ripped from their sockets and sent off to the Harris Museum in Preston. They were replaced with the same lack of attention by posts of characterless concrete. Though only the sockets now remain Bleasdale still has a haunting atmosphere.

Woodhenges are very uncommon, there are only two others in Europe; one is near Cologne on the Rhine and the second not far from Stonehenge in Wiltshire. The Bleasdale timber circle must therefore be one of the greatest losses to both archaeology and the tourist industry; such remarkable monuments should never again be treated in so cavalier a fashion.

BOLTON

In Bolton almost everyone passes Lord Derby's column in Churchgate but a survey conducted for a television company showed that out of 50 passers-by only two correctly identified the column and knew its significance.

The Derby connection begins at the hostelry 'Ye Olde Man and Scythe' where the inscription on a wall plaque reads 'James Stanley, seventh Earl of Derby, spent the last few hours of his life in the Inn previous to his execution'. This took place on October 15th 1651 at the market cross a few yards away. The column now marks the spot where the executioner George Whewell's axe fell on Derby's neck (See also *Affetside*), and the chair on which he sat prior to his execution still remains in 'Ye. Olde Man and Scythe'.

Derby's execution was more important than most others of the period when many Cavaliers met their end because of their opposition to Parliament. There is some truth in the oft quoted jest that Roundheads were Right but Repulsive whilst the Cavaliers were Wrong but Romantic. None was more wrong than Lord Derby and none met their end more romantically.

During the Civil War the Royalists under the command of Lord Stanley, aided by Prince Rupert and 10,000 troops, swept into Bolton. The town which had strong Parliamentarian sympathies was sacked by the troops, many citizens were needlessly slaughtered and thereafter the survivors hated the Royalist leaders especially Lord Derby, who like them was a Lancastrian.

Charles I was executed in 1649 and his son Charles II was defeated at Worcester in 1651 as he tried to retain the throne. The king escaped by hiding in the famous oak tree at Boscobel but Lord Derby was captured and there was only one place where he could be sent to be executed – Bolton.

Once his head had been severed the family were allowed to have his remains for burial. Lord Derby died only one death, has only one monument to mark the fatal spot, but he has two coffins in Ormskirk church – one for his head the other, obviously much larger, which contains his body.

*   *   *

Crompton Way carries a continual stream of traffic through Bolton's bypass, but few know that the name celebrates the achievements of Samuel Crompton one of the pioneers of the cotton industry.

Two buildings are now separated by Crompton Way – Firwood Fold on one side and Hall i'th' Wood on the other. They were once linked by a meandering woodland path. Samuel Crompton, the inventor of the Spinning Mule, was born in 1753 in a thatched cottage which still survives at Firwood Fold. He lived there with his family until they moved to the 16th-century half-timbered manor house known locally as Hall i'th' Wood (the hall set in the wood). This move did not mean that the Cromptons had suddenly become wealthy, but rather the reverse. The hall was in a sad state of repair and was divided into a number of tenements used as a work-cum-living area for handloom weavers.

Samuel was a hard working lad and in 1779 he began to produce a spinning machine (later called his mule) which was eventually to revolutionise the textile industry. His fellow handloom weavers did not take kindly to Samuel's machine which could produce the work of six. Angry weavers armed with hammers made short work of young Sam's machine and he therefore took to subterfuge. High in the rafters of the hall he laboured long into the night and to his sin of 'taking the bread from the mouths of bairns was added the even worse outrage of dabbling in the occult at midnight!'

Samuel Crompton may have been an inventor bordering on genius but as a businessman he was a disaster. He made fortunes for others but on his death he had 'nowt but £63'. His grave is in St Peter's church cemetery but his birthplace is not revered as befits the man who crowned King Cotton.

Hall i'th' Wood fell on even harder times after Crompton's tenement was vacated and it was only saved from demolition by another famous son of Bolton. This was William Hesketh Lever who became Lord Leverhulme and founded the Port Sunlight empire. He restored Hall i'th' Wood and gave it to Bolton as a museum.

A few of Samuel Crompton's possessions are on display in the museum including his watch, walking stick, tobacco pouch and especially a violin bow which he made in 1770. He also made his own wind operated organ proving that the lad from Firwood Fold was something of a mechanical all-rounder.

*   *   *

Smithills Hall on the outskirts of Bolton is a magnificent half-timbered medieval manor house, but not listed often enough on the tourist trail even by those who specialise in ghost hunting. My introduction to the hall began in the 1960s on my first day as a schoolmaster at the local grammar school where the morning service was held in the chapel of the hall. As a newcomer I was shown around the building and remarked that I felt chilly. My guide said 'I'm not surprised, you are standing close to the Martyr's footprint'.

Born the son of a farmer in the nearby village of Deane, the Revd George Marsh (1515-1555) was unusual in the sense that he became a Protestant martyr. In the reign of Bloody Mary Tudor, George refused point blank to temper his Protestantism and Justice Barton 'examined' the priest in the Green Chamber of Smithills Hall. The trial, if such it could be termed, developed into a fierce debate of ecclesiastical doctrine and George Marsh got so angry that he stamped his foot with such force that the mark was ever afterwards imprinted upon the flagged floor.

George Marsh was taken first to Lord Derby's house at Lathom, then to Lancaster Castle and finally to Chester where he was burned at the stake. The footprint which, it was once said, dripped with blood is now well signed and I have spoken to others who felt that George Marsh's presence will be forever with us.

Smithhills Hall is now a fine museum having been carefully restored in 1994 and the old coaching house is a restaurant. Its courtyard contains a number of restored coaches and the old stables are easily recognisable.

The whole estate is surrounded by mature woodlands in which nature walks have been established. There one can sit among the trees looking out at the hall and beyond it the village of Deane, now a suburb of Bolton. How long did it take the locals to be allowed to remember the Martyr who stamped his foot at Bloody Mary? One guess might be at the time of the Armada when Elizabeth did a bit of Protestant stamping on her own account!

BOLTON-BY-BOWLAND

The most attractive feature of any English village is its green, and so what can be said about Bolton-by-Bowland which has two? The larger green is fringed by trees on one side, and the other by an assortment of attractive and well proportioned buildings constructed of local stone. It seems, however, that the smaller and less obvious green may have been the focal point of the old village, and it is here that we find the broken stump of the old market cross and also the posts which once supported the stocks. These are overlooked by the church of St Peter and St Paul which is neatly sandwiched between the two greens.

Inside the church is a memorial to Sir Ralph Pudsay and his three wives. Oh yes, his 25 children are also commemorated. I'll bet the sculptor didn't land too many commissions as good as this one! On the slab of limestone all 29 individuals are carved. These include Sir Ralph and his wives Matilda, Margaret and Edwina. On the lower folds of the ladies' dresses the number of children they bore are carved in Roman numerals. The statistics of six and two are not startling but Edwina's 17 was remarkable especially in the days of high infant mortality. The children and the names of each are also carved upon this remarkable slab.

A staunch supporter of the Lancastrian side during the Wars of the Roses, Sir Ralph concealed King Henry VI after his defeat at Hexham in 1464. Poor Henry seems to have visited a number of villages in the Clitheroe area, but was so harrassed by his enemies that he was kept constantly on the move.

The Pudsay family seems to have had its share of eccentrics, not least the one who made the famous leap. Towards the end of the 16th century, William Pudsay, who was renowned for his lavish hospitality, ran short of money and the story goes that he took himself off for a ride into the woods to have a quiet think. Here he met a bunch of fairies who gave him a magic bit for his horse. This bit was supposed to provide any horse wearing it with superior strength. He also followed up a hint that if he dug a mine at Skelhorn (now known as the site of the disused Rimington lead mines) he would find silver. The facts indicate that Pudsay did find silver and set up a mint of his own which produced Pudsay shillings. All went well until the authorities got wind of the illegal currency. Legend says that, as the law approached, Pudsay grabbed the magic bit, saddled up and galloped off pursued by the officers. It was then that his horse leapt over the Ribble above Sawley at a point still called Pudsay's leap. Much more likely is that Pudsay got away with a caution because he had made no attempt to conceal his coins or copy any existing currency, even engraving his own mark of 'an escollop'. It also helped that Queen Elizabeth I was his godmother and William travelled south and knelt at her feet asking for forgiveness.

The Rimington complex was made a 'mine royal', the family never being allowed to mine there again, and after the Civil War they sold the land. Despite old Sir Ralph's virility the family ran out of male heirs and the line ended with the death of Bridget Pudsay in 1770. The family line may have disappeared but it is commemorated by one of the most interesting tombs in Britain, a magnificent monument which receives far too few visitors.

 ## BORWICK

A detour of less than two miles from the A6 Kendal to Carnforth road leads to this small, leafy hamlet dominated by its magnificent Tudor hall. The earliest building is the ivy-clad, 14th-century defensive pele tower which consists of four storeys. A delightful baronial hall was dovetailed into the tower during the late 16th-century after peace had been made between England and Scotland and the need for a defensive house had passed. Borwick was the home of the Bindloss family and whilst they were not a major force in the country they were related to most of the important families in Northern England. Sir Robert Bindloss is famous for being the last person in the area to stock his kitchen by means of an employed falconer and also for entertaining Charles II during his futile attempt to reclaim his throne in 1651.

The Bindloss estate at Borwick was notoriously rich and Sir Robert needed no fewer than 24 tythe barns to store the produce of his farms. One of these remains and as the house is unspoiled Tudor it deserves to be much better known.

The nine acres of grounds include woodlands and formal gardens. Borwick Hall is now a residential training centre, but it is open to the public for three weeks during August. There are, however, excellent views of it from the village, and down by the bridge is another old barn once used as a night-halt by travellers along the cattle drove roads from the breeding grounds in Scotland to the lucrative markets of southern England.

BRADSHAW

Bradshaw was once a village of some importance but now a suburb of Bolton and set on the Burnley Road. Approaching from Burnley is a T-junction controlled by traffic lights. Straight ahead is a stout tower which is all that remains of the 15th century church dedicated to St Maxentius. This is the only church in England to be dedicated to a saint who lived in 6th century France and was famous for his relationship with birds (feathered).

Perhaps the serenity which surrounded him and enabled him to charm wildlife saved his life. When heathen hordes threatened his abbey Maxentius walked out to meet them. As they were about to hack him to death with their swords the heathens were said to have been overawed by his holiness and to have fallen to their knees, begged his forgiveness and became Christians.

Perhaps those who began the demolition of the old church got the same feeling and spared the tower.

BROUGHTON

The modern complex network of roads has tended to submerge some of our ancient villages beneath a sea of concrete and tarmac. One of the worst affected has been Broughton, sandwiched between the A6, the M6 and the M55 motorways just on the outskirts of Preston.

The name Broughton is probably derived from the Saxon 'Broctun' meaning a settlement constructed around a farm and a brook. Archaeologists have discovered the site of the old village set around Blundell Brook which flows just to the south of the church, dedicated to St John the Baptist.

The church is a real mixture of ancient and modern taking us back to the time when Broughton village stood at the junction of tracks dating to prehistoric times. There was probably a wooden church at Broughton in Saxon times, but the present building is mainly 19th century although its strong tower dates to 1533, when the threat of invasion from Scotland was great. Church towers in the north of medieval England had to be built to be as strong as castles.

Opposite the church is the school and behind it is a thatched building restored in 1995 but once part of the Church Inn which was closed around 1870, becoming the home of the sexton. By this time the focus of the village had shifted to the present line along the A6 straddling the line of the turnpike road linking Preston and Lancaster.

Even though Broughton always seems busy with traffic a slow stroll along the main street can still be an unexpectedly enthralling history lesson. Pinfold Cottage is a reminder of the time stray sheep and cattle from the surrounding farms were penned to await being claimed by their owners.

Almost next door is the old Toll Bar cottage built in the late 18th century to collect the tolls from the through traffic. Local historians have discovered that charges were not cheap – a horse, a landau and even a sledge in snow or a hearse on its way to church had to pay the then considerable sum of sixpence to pass through the gate (called a turnpike) which barred the road. The wet surrounding fields made it almost impossible to go round the gate. Oh yes – soldiers, loads of manure and politicians could pass through without charge!

'Time Warp' villages like Broughton should persuade those who speed along our motorways to take more time over their journey. Only then is it possible to discover the secret places of our countryside.

BROWSHOLME HALL

One of the most underated of Lancashire's halls is Browsholme (pronounced Brews and meaning a hill) which is folded into a secluded area of the Hodder valley. Hidden by its gardens and woodlands Browsholme is reached via a gatehouse and drive and the first sight of the house is breathtaking in its beauty.

The Parker family have been at Browsholme since the 14th century and the present hall was built in 1507 but refaced in attractive red sandstone in 1604. The gardens are a riot of colour in summer and within are a few pieces of priceless stained glass which were removed from Whalley Abbey when it was dissolved in 1537.

With regard to the history of the Forest of Bowland which surrounds the hall the most interesting artefact is a gauge which was once used to measure dogs. Nobody without due authority was allowed to keep a dog large enough to hunt deer. Any dog which could not pass through the gauge was deemed too large and either had to be killed or have its legs mutilated so that it could not pursue its quarry. Deer were not just hunted for fun as it was a case of providing fresh meat for the lord of the manor.

Browsholme is open to the public during the summer but above all it is a family home and has been for five centuries.

BRUNGERLEY

────── There are few more historic spots in Lancashire than Brungerley, between Clitheroe and Waddington, and yet its story is almost lost in the mists of time.

The Wars of the Roses meant that the latter part of the 15th century was in almost constant turmoil. Henry VI fared particularly badly and following his defeat at Hexham in Northumberland in 1464 he fled to his friends in Lancashire. He stayed for a while at Waddington Hall under the protection of the Tempest family. The hall, still in private hands, stands just off the main street of the village.

The Talbots, another influential family, supported the Yorkist cause of Edward IV and once they knew his whereabouts Henry VI was again on the run. He apparently had to leave his dinner half eaten on the table and flee for his life.

In the days before the bridge was constructed at Brungerley the Ribble could only be crossed via a substantial set of stepping stones – known locally as the Hippings – and the King was caught whilst negotiating this hazard. He was taken to London where he was imprisoned in the Tower. There he spent five years before being replaced on the throne by the Earl of Warwick in 1471, captured at Barnet the following year, and murdered in the Tower.

Until 1801 the stones and the rather deep ford used by horses and carts were the only ways across but events downstream made the construction of a bridge absolutely vital. To provide the Clitheroe textile mills with water a dam was constructed at Edisford and the water backing up from this raised the level of the river at Brungerley and submerged the Hipping stones. The first bridge was not a success and was replaced by the present structure in 1816 although this has had to be widened several times since.

During the last war several temporary bridges were built by the Royal Engineers who trained men here prior to sending them to the war in Europe where bridges had to be repaired or built from scratch at great speed. Some of the concrete supports of the apprentice engineers' efforts can still be found in a tangle of riverside vegetation which includes butterbur.

The Brungerley butterbur is no common species but the very rare white variety *Petasites alba*. Local people following the pleasant footpath along the Ribble to West Bradford seldom notice this botanical treasure of Brungerley. Nor do they realise that in the early 1900s rowing boats could be hired and on pleasant summer days this was a popular pleasure ground.

On most days of the year it is possible to enjoy this tranquil place all on your own. Look down at the Hippings and think of the capture of an English king. If you are very lucky a kingfisher will skim under the bridge or a patient heron will perch on the stones waiting for an unwary fish.

 ## BURNLEY

────── Overlooking the Leeds to Liverpool Canal and Pendle Water the Barden Lane area of Burnley was once famous for an Easter celebration which is still affectionately known as Jack Moore's Monkey.

Until the 1960s Good Friday was busy down Barden Lane and stalls were set up alongside the road by the canal and riverside and Jack Moore, the local farmer sold ice-cream and minerals in his barn. Close to where he operated his swing-boats he kept a monkey to amuse the holiday makers. Rowing boats were hired along the canal and everyone had fun buying toy monkeys on a string and other novelties and ate ginger-bread, roast potatoes and black peas. The latter is a Lancashire delicacy which is making something of a comeback in a few local markets where they once sold succulent toffee apples and sticks of rock.

The Easter celebrations have now faded into history, but although the origin is forgotten the farm and barn are still known as Jack Moore's Monkey.

Alongside the Leeds to Liverpool Canal as it enfolds itself around Burnley is one of the wonders of the Canal Age which receives no publicity. Even the Weavers Triangle Heritage Centre, although being restored from 1996 onwards, is given scant recognition of its historical significance.

The Weavers Triangle is a new name for an old industrial complex of warehouses set around the canal. Some mistakenly say the whole area is triangular in shape but the truth is that each mill had a huge iron triangle and a metal bar. The two were brought into sharp and strident contact, making them easily audible among the clatter of the working looms whenever a fire was threatened. This was thus Burnley's early warning system.

The Weavers Triangle Heritage Centre is a splendid little museum tucked away beneath a tangle of busy roads and based in the old canal toll house and the dwelling of the wharf master. This is now full of artefacts dealing with the town but especially the Leeds to Liverpool Canal which was fully opera-tional from around 1810.

The Straight Mile embankment is actually only around two thirds of a mile, but one shudders to think what the locals will say if and when the Europeans insist on the stretch going metric. The engineering marvel soars high above the town and it is possible to look down on the glass roofs which allowed the weavers in the mills to keep working until the last rays of sunlight had faded.

Steps from the Straight Mile lead down into the car park of Sainsbury's supermarket. There among the trolleys are a couple of lime kilns which the authorities have left in situ. These relate to the time when limestone was delivered by canal and used to burn the material essential to produce mortar, needed in huge volume as Burnley developed from an agricultural village into a cotton town.

Nearby is the old Tudor grammar school, the town well and the market cross. Here then we have a little known industrial gem overlooking a historic village, both almost but not quite swamped by a modern town.

*   *   *

The town's art gallery and museum, Towneley Hall is rated as one of the most important medieval manor houses in Lancashire and is open free of charge daily except Saturdays. Its old stables have been converted into a café, the estate's brew house into a craft centre and the gardens now form part of a nature centre.

In the grounds of the hall are two structures which are often overlooked. At the junction of the nature trails is the medieval Foldys Cross which was once a focus for Christian travellers, and in an even more isolated situation is one of the best preserved ice houses to be found in England.

Ice houses were essential in the days when refrigerators were unheard of. A deep hole was dug and then surrounded by an igloo shaped (significant perhaps) stone building. During the winter ice was collected from ponds and lakes, brought to the ice house and wrapped in hay to insulate it; unless the summer was particularly hot a supply of ice could be guaranteed for at least 12 months.

BURSCOUGH PRIORY

——— Of all Lancashire's religious houses Burscough seems to have been the most harshly treated. So much of this gem has been lost that its former magnificence is hard to appreciate.

Opposite the Bull and Dog inn just outside Ormskirk on the busy A59 road, a narrow lane leads down to the railway line and across this is a farm. Burscough Priory's scanty ruins are almost swamped by the farm and its outbuildings. Two pillars, a central arch of the church and a wall or two are all that remains of the monastic settlement.

Burscough was founded in 1124 for the Black Canons of the Augustinian order by Robert Fitz Henry de Lathom. When in its prime the house had one of the most remarkable chapter houses, some magnificent stained glass and a floor expensively laid with glazed tiles. A leper hospital was attached to the complex but at a discreet distance from the church.

The priory was important enough to be chosen as the last resting place of the Stanley family. In the Burscough vaults were the remains of Lord Stanley who took the crown from the body of Richard III following the battle of Bosworth in 1485 and placed it on the head of Henry VII. Actually Thomas Lord Stanley was the second husband of Margaret of Richmond, mother of Henry. Following his victory the new king visited the Stanleys at nearby Lathom and came to Burscough to give thanks for his victory.

The priory was dissolved in 1536 with many of its stones and furniture being moved to nearby Ormskirk. The church had a steeple but around 1540 a tower was added to house the bells from Burscough. This fact has failed to displace the legend which suggests that the spire was built by a rich spinster and the tower by her sister determined not to be outdone!

Some of the Stanley effigies were also transferred to Ormskirk and one battered stone figure may be that dedicated to Margaret of Richmond herself. The King's Choir in the church was named after Henry VII.

The peal which once called the brethren of Burscough to prayer was saved at Ormskirk whilst the priory ruins have to make do with the sound of cattle, sheep and wild birds such as curlew and lapwing. Perhaps this is not such a bad swap!

BURTON-IN-KENDAL

——— Before the coming of the railway, which put nearby Carnforth on the map, the old coach road from Preston to Lancaster went through Burton-in-Kendal. Now an isolated backwater held in a timewarp, it has nevertheless retained all the atmosphere of its days as a small coaching town.

As reminders of the coaching era are magnificent old inns including the Kings Arms, at the rear of which are the old stables. Their walls are hanging with luxuriant growths of spleenwort fern, used long ago in the treatment of diseases of the spleen, but there is no scientific evidence that it ever worked.

Burton once held an important corn market and its square is dominated by an 18th century cross. Life was not all peace and tranquillity as proven by the steps of the cross which bear the remains of leg irons to which wrong-doers were attached.

CARTFORD BRIDGE

—— Until 1993 two toll bridges crossed the river Wyre; following the demolition of Shard Bridge only Cartford Bridge remains. By the time the bridge has been crossed and the small toll paid, motorists have only just changed gear as they whizz pass a real gem without a second glance.

Wild Boar Cottage was once a café but it is now a private residence easily seen from the road without disturbing the owners. A carriage, looking like a tramcar, but which was once carried around on Blackpool's Big Wheel or Ferris Wheel as it was known, has been snuggly dovetailed into the cottage.

The carriage is here because of the kindness of two sisters named Swallow who ran the Blackpool orphanage and had their private home at Wild Boar Cottage. This, originally intended for farm workers, had been constructed using local bricks made from the clay dug out when making a pond for farm animals, long since filled in. When Blackpool's Ferris Wheel was demolished in 1928 the sisters bought one of the carriages, had it transported by horse and cart and joined it to their cottage. This allowed them the extra space needed to give the orphans a free holiday with the girls sleeping in the carriage and the boys in a tent in the garden.

The Swallow sisters continued to care for those less fortunate than themselves throughout the 1930s. Some time ago a radio programme about the Swallows and the Ferris Wheel carriage brought letters from orphans who had been entertained by the sisters, and their memories helped breathe life into an unforgettable and heart-warming chapter in Lancashire's history.

CASTERCLIFFE

—— The magnificent Iron Age forts of Dorset and the West Country rather overshadow those in other parts of the country.

They also often have the advantage of being close to busy tourist centres. It therefore comes as a surprise to discover a fine example of an Iron Age camp on an isolated hillside on the old road between Colne and Nelson.

Looming over a small farmhouse and serenaded in summer by the song of soaring skylarks, Castercliffe is thought to have been active around 200 BC, and Roman coins found nearby suggest that the legionnaries later used it to keep an eye on the Calder Valley. Archaeological evidence indicates that the hill fortifications were never actually completed.

It seems likely that Castercliffe remained in splendid isolation until the 14th century when coal was discovered among the surrounding outcroppings and was mined under licence by the monks from Bolton Priory in Wharfedale.

Local tradition suggests that there was once a 'mighty castle' at Castercliffe which was totally destroyed by the Cromwellians during the Civil War. Although this is highly unlikely, cannon balls have been discovered nearby which prove that there was some conflict centred around the area.

The peace and tranquillity of Castercliffe, however, has not been disturbed for nearly four centuries and it shows.

CATLOW BOTTOMS

Catlow Bottoms, near Nelson, has a very much under-rated treasure – its packhorse bridge.

Because of the hills of Lancashire packhorse routes survived longer than in many other parts of England. Not only are the tracks themselves of interest but so are the bridges which crossed rivers and streams. In the first instance travellers crossed streams by fords, but these were unreliable in wet weather and when the snow on the hills began to melt.

Bridges became essential and at first they were just tree trunks or slabs of stone placed across the water. These, however, were not suitable for teams of horses and from the 14th century onwards delightfully humped packhorse bridges developed. Some of the most famous of these are in the north of England and have been well documented and preserved.

Before roads were built in the damp valley below Catlow Bottoms bridge stood at the crossroads of two vital routes, one between Colne and Burnley and the other connecting Clitheroe with Halifax. This ancient highway and its bridge are now overgrown with grass and bracken, but its route can still be followed and it is easy to imagine the packhorses following the same route. They travelled in trains (which is how the railway term originated) of between 20 and 40 animals organised by a driver assisted by a couple of attendants. The leading horse wore a collar festooned with bells.

These were specially made in Wigan and their notes were unique to each train and could also be operated to indicate to the intelligent horses towards the rear whether their leader was turning right or left. Approaching trains could also hear others coming and the sound of the bells prevented chaos on these narrow roads. Memories survived long after the packhorses had been replaced by canals, railways and better roads and in the early years of this century children in the Catlow district and in other areas played a game called 'bell horses'.

The bridge is almost always deserted but sitting close to its graceful arch it is easy to imagine the bells, the sound of the hooves, the clank of the saddle straps and the urging of the man in charge of the train. Vital commodities passed this way including wheat, limestone, coal, iron ore, textiles and anything which needed transporting and was within the carrying capacity of the horses, each of which could cope with two hundredweights for up to 20 miles a day.

CATON

'Blink and tha'll miss it' was the warning given by a Lunesdale farmer when asked the way to Caton. Refrain from blinking and you will find a piece of Lancashire's history overlooked not only by tourists but also literally by the Druids' Oak, a dead and twisted oak which provides the folklore but, even though old it cannot possibly date back to the Druids. Its bent and time battered trunk almost curls around a well preserved set of fish stones joined together by metal ties.

The fishing rights on the nearby river Lune belonged to the monks of Furness Abbey who also had a farm nearby. Obviously the monks provided for their own needs first but any surplus fish, mainly salmon and trout, were laid on the fish stones and sold off to the local people who gathered there to await the arrival of their next meal.

Old Caton is now joined by a sprawl of new houses to Brockhouse, which has a splendid old bridge. Built into its fabric is a plague stone, a rare survivor of the devasting Black Death of the late 14th century, an epidemic caused by a virus transmitted to man by fleas from migrating Asian black rats. Those infected by the disease still needed to eat, but also had to be isolated from those not infected. Bakers and butchers and perhaps even those trading from the fish stones placed their goods on the bridge and the money was dropped into a hollow in the stone, which was filled with vinegar. The people of the time could not be sure that this method prevented cross infection, perhaps the doctors or herbalists of the day had tentatively suggested it as a prophylactic measure, but there is no doubt that it worked.

CHIPPING

——— Chipping, with its lovely old cottages and inns dominated by the church of St Bartholomew, takes its name from the Saxon word for a market. It is still a busy village with a number of pretty tea shops, one of which is now also the post office and craft shop. A plaque on the wall informs us that here was once the shop, office and home of the Quaker John Brabin who died in 1683.

The shopkeeper has a copy of John Brabin's will which provided money for the provision of alms-houses and a well-appointed grammar school which still stand in splendid condition, the school being a great rarity in the history of Lancashire villages.

John made his fortune as a dyer and cloth merchant and the main street has altered little since the blue-coated Brabin scholars strolled along it to commune with their master who lived in an adjacent house. This was also funded by the founder. High standards were set and in his will Brabin ordered that any master 'falling short' should be instantly 'put out' by the governors.

Chipping is within a short stroll of a fast moving brook which once powered mills, one of which is now the base of the Berry's chair factory specialising in traditional rush chairs

Brabin's Grammar School.

which have been made here for several centuries. Tweedies Mill has now gone but until the 1950s it manufactured ship portholes from the days when Thomas Lipton built tea clippers in the days of sail.

Leagram Hall, now a private residence, is reached along a beautiful footpath and yet is almost unknown even to local walkers. Leagram began as a medieval deer park, and many of the splendid trees including some oaks would have been well known to John Wild, a fine naturalist who kept detailed diaries of his observations between 1850 and 1886. In September 1856 he reported a swallow which was 'dull white without a single coloured feather about it, the eye was black with a beautiful bright yellow rim encircling it'. This, the albino swallow, was a rare event not only in Lancashire but also in the world of natural history.

CHORLEY

Chorley may seem to be a town created by the Industrial Revolution, but just like all the mill towns, it has more than its share of history and beauty whilst also producing a number of famous folk.

To a son of Chorley we owe the sugar cube and the Tate Gallery which often exhibits its own version of modern 'cubism'. Henry Tate was born in Chorley in 1819 and his first job was as a grocer's assistant. Always an ambitious person Tate developed his own business concerned with the import of sugar first through Liverpool and then through London. Tate provided money for the famous art gallery which has recently expanded its operations to Liverpool.

Every old town should have a grand old house and in Astley Hall Chorley has one of the best although less well known than similar houses. Astley is on the site of a Bronze Age burial mound and an inscribed stone almost hidden near the car park marks the actual spot.

The hall and the well-wooded park which surrounds it was given to the town in 1922. Initially a half-timbered Tudor house it was the home of three famous families. First came the Charnocks, then the Brookes family who originated at Mere and then the Towneley-Parker family.

The typically Tudor home was drastically altered in 1666 to produce a Jacobean dwelling somewhat reminiscent of Hardwick Hall in Derbyshire. Both these buildings can be difficult to photograph because they contain so much glass that the frontage gleams whenever the sun is shining and at times the reflection can be almost blinding.

The hall is open to the public on payment of a fee, but in winter care should be taken to check the opening times. There is a large car park, and the grounds are always open; through them runs a splendid nature trail. The old stable-block has been converted into a pleasant little café. Even in winter Astley Park looks a joy with some flowers still adding splashes of colour. The cast iron drinking fountain opposite the path leading to the stable café is a triumph of the design techniques of a bygone age. There is plenty to see inside the hall, in particular the truly magnificent plaster ceilings and a fine example of a shovelboard which is more than 20 ft long and supported on ten pairs of stout wooden legs. Shovelboard was once a very popular game rather like shove-halfpenny but this example used large coins which were moved by maces almost like snooker-cues. This game is situated in the long gallery which runs along the front of the house.

Among its other attractions Astley therefore has two special features; the site of a Bronze Age settlement and a long-forgotten indoor game.

CLAUGHTON

—— As Claughton, sometimes confused with Claughton-on-Brock, is a rather unattractive village between Lancaster and Kirkby Lonsdale, it is tempting to ignore it, but this would be a grave error. No other village has its manor house split into two, the Tudor section being moved uphill leaving the 17th century section on the original site and serving as a farmhouse. Nobody seems to know the reason for this architectural split but it has been suggested that it was due to a family quarrel.

Near the Tudor section is a modern church with an ancient bell, inscribed 1296, which is accepted as the oldest named bell in England, although a few other bells suspected of being earlier do not carry a date.

CLIFTON MILL

—— For many years the Fylde was affectionately known as Windmill Land. Some of its many windmills still stand alone and aloof and are well known whilst many others have sadly disappeared for ever. Clifton Mill fits into neither of these categories and has been almost but not quite hidden by extensions attached to it during its conversion first into a dwelling and later into a pub. It stands almost on the line of the old Roman road.

The mill originally had six storeys and was first built in the 1600s although much altered in the years which followed. Those who complain about the sacrilege of converting the building should be reminded of the fate of the majority of the Fylde's windmills which have long since been demolished. It may not be grinding wheat for bread but Clifton Mill is still catering well for the inner man.

The precise history of the mill is something of a mystery and there is another puzzle, a monument almost hidden in the bank on the opposite side of the road. This may be a boundary stone, preaching cross or a place to rest coffins carried to church for burial. It could well be that the monument once served all three functions, but now it stands functionless and almost forgotten.

The top of the monument is not original but placed there in 1913 in the memory of Edmund Birley of Clifton Hall. Anyone who fails to notice this cross can be forgiven because of the nearby towering bulk of the Springfield works of British Nuclear Fuels which first opened in 1945.

CLITHEROE SPA

—— Clitheroe is the second oldest borough in Lancashire (Wigan is the most ancient), and its charter dates to 1147. It is one of the most popular areas in the Ribble valley, and the town and its surroundings have a goodly number of interesting buildings, including the castle, which ensure a regular stream of visitors. It has others, however, which are generally missed.

Within a short distance of the town centre are fascinating reminders of Clitheroe's history, all of which are usually passed by locals and visitors without so much as a second glance. Below the Grammar School is St Mary's Well, one of the three old town water supplies although there were also a number of springs typical of limestone areas.

At one time Clitheroe almost developed into a spa town to rival Harrogate or Buxton. Evidence of the old spa can still be seen on the Pendleside outskirts of the town now partly occupied by houses. The spa had a classically designed frontage, gritstone arcades and corbels. The use of these springs, which smell strongly of sulphur, may well predate the advertisment in the *Blackburn Daily Mail* of 1838 which described the spa buildings as neat and offering hot and cold baths, healing waters, dressing rooms and other 'convenient apartments'. The idea of a Clitheroe Spa was the brainchild of Stephen Embly who also built an ale-house known as the Stop and Rest which was later converted to three cottages which stand at the foot of Claremont Brow. The waters were recommended for healing not only humans but also animals.

In the 1850s the nearby village of Grindleton also had a spa and this is now part of a school. Here were both sulphur and lime springs which boasted an impressive list of clients. The old Hydro Lodge still stands on the left of the road leading to Gisburn. Taking 'mineral waters' was then a recognised cure for many skin complaints including leprosy.

Clitheroe once had its own 12th century leper hospital but this had long gone by the time attempts were being made to set up the commercial spa.

CLIVIGER

The valiant Light Brigade galloped into the Valley of Death and inspired Tennyson's famous poem but have you ever wondered what happened to the Heavy Brigade? To discover the answer you need to visit the tiny little churchyard of St John's at Cliviger situated between Burnley and Todmorden.

Here is the grave of General Scarlett, an unsung hero of the battle of Balaclava which was fought on 25th October 1854. Scarlett became aware that the forces at the British rear were in danger of being isolated by a determined Russian assault. He galloped his troops around the back of a hill and emerged with about 300 men almost into the direct line of 3,000 Russian cavalry. He should have retreated but instead he charged and either frightened the Russians or overwhelmed them with surprise at his stupidity. Had it not been for the fate of the equally gallant Light Brigade, Scarlett's charge would have been famous rather than almost totally forgotten.

Scarlett even made a last ditch charge to support the Light Brigade but was recalled by the bugle of Lord Lucan who, after having relayed the order for the ill-fated charge, decided that he could not afford to lose the Heavy Brigade as well. Scarlett lived at Bank Hall in Burnley which for a while served as the town's Maternity Hospital. His sword and regalia are on display in Towneley Hall Museum, Burnley. His grave at Cliviger is close to the open moorlands and caressed by breezes, blasted by winds, and stands four square against the elements. No brave general could ask for more and he may even welcome the solitude of his almost unknown grave.

From Lancaster, take the A588 and continue to Upper Thurnham. Opposite Thurnham Hall turn right and follow the road signed to a lighthouse and Cockersand Abbey. There is a small car park at Cockerham Sands.

A short stroll along the coast leads to Cockersand Abbey. Some of the stones of the monastery are now incorporated into a farmhouse and a disused lighthouse stands guard over a vast expanse of sand, whilst the sound of sea birds fills the air. The road beyond the abbey farm ends at the Wyre/Lune Bird Sanctuary which is very popular with birds but surprisingly little known to birdwatchers.

Looking at the abbey site today it is difficult to imagine that of the 20 or so monasteries which existed in Lancashire, Cockersand was third in wealth and wielded great influence. It began life as a hermitage but by the time of Henry II (1154-1189) it had been 'up-graded' to a hospital for aged monks from an abbey as far away as Leicester. They must surely have enjoyed their last days in this idyllic spot. William de Lancaster, Baron of Kendal and also the Fleming family were generous in giving land to the abbey, including Pilling Moss with its wealth of winter wildfowl, especially greylag and pink-footed geese. This led in the year 1190 to Pope Clement ordaining the house under the name of the Monastery of St Mary of the Premonstratensian Order of Cockersand. Gifts continued to pour in and by 1290 the monks held almost 100 tracts of land, some of them very substantial and from which the rents must have been considerable. This did not stop the crafty brethren from pleading poverty and asking Richard II for financial assistance to repair flood damage. They told him that 'The sea has now washed the bones of the monks out of their cemetery'.

Cockersand was dissolved along with the other monastic houses in Lancashire in 1537, but was granted the rare privilege of a re-foundation; this only lasted two years and then the Royal Commissioners broke the abbey seal. The plate and jewels belonging to the monks were taken for the king; the furniture and goods were sold – some can still be found in several other places of Lancashire.

The abbot's lodging and the offices were left standing, but the church, the cloisters and the dwellings of the monks were stripped of the lead which protected them from the weather, and of every other saleable object, and left to fall into ruins. The site was leased by the Crown to John and Robert Gardner of Pilling, and five years afterwards was passed on to John Kitchen of Pilling Hall. Only the chapter house now remains, this having been preserved solely because it was used as a burial place by the Dalton family of Thurnham Hall. In a nearby farm are a number of relics from the monastery and the owners showed me round pointing out Early English windows in the cow shed, and ornately carved stones in the old privy.

The Dalton family buried at Cockersand will surely have found peace in a spot overlooking the sea and lulled by the sound of birds.

 ## COLNE

—— Since a new purpose-built structure was opened in the town centre Colne's former library has become a Unitarian chapel.

In the front garden, next to Albert Road, is what is best described as a mini-history lesson but now becoming overgrown and unknown to all save a faithful few. Almost smothered by shrubbery is one of the early gas lamps which illuminated Victorian Colne and also the foundation stone of the Cloth Hall which co-ordinated the woollen trade of the town before the textile mills sprouted and cotton became king.

The most evocative feature, however, is a memorial bust to local man Wallace Hartley who was the bandmaster on board the ill-fated *Titanic*. She sank on 15th April 1912 with the loss of 1,490 lives. As she slipped beneath the waves it was Wallace who struck up the tune 'Nearer My God to Thee' and whose bravery touched the heart of the nation.

COWAN BRIDGE

—— Despite being directly on the A65 road linking Ingleton and Kirkby Lonsdale, Cowan Bridge, seems on the surface at least, to have nothing to delay the tourist. Here, however, is an important link in the story of the famous Brontë family. Pause for a while in the village and just over the bridge find a row of now privately owned cottages. On the wall nearest to the roadside is a stone tablet inscribed:

"At this school Maria, Elizabeth, Charlotte, Emily, daughters of the Rev. P. Brontë were educated in 1824-25."

This was a Clergy Daughters' School run by the austere and humourless Revd W. Carus Wilson. The school still exists, although now well thought of and transferred to Casterton between Kirkby Lonsdale and Sedburgh.

Their time at Cowan Bridge was far from happy for the Brontë girls and Charlotte used her loathing of the place in *Jane Eyre* but changed its name to Lowood. She also used the Revd Carus Wilson as the prototype for Mr Brocklehurst. After a bout of fever which led to the death of Maria and Elizabeth, Charlotte and Emily were allowed to return to Haworth. There were, however, a few bright spots including the footpath across the fields from the school to the Revd Carus Wilson's parish church at Tunstall. This path can still be followed and is a delight in spring with curlew and larks adding their voice to the chuckling of several streams.

CRAWSHAWBOOTH

—— The village, which straddles the A56 between Manchester and Burnley just beyond Rawtenstall, looks industrial and uninteresting. The ancient centre, however, is situated down in the valley of Limey Water, a tributary of the Irwell. A humpbacked bridge on an old packhorse route crosses the stream and a track leads off over the moors to Haslingden. In the days when the valley sides were full of trees and the bottoms flooded, the only reliable trade routes kept to the well-drained hill tops. The handloom weavers' cottages can still be seen upon the hillsides. The view from the moorland is magnificent and must have provided the travellers of old with an idea of where the local thugs might try to attack and rob them.

Near the packhorse bridge is an animal cemetery where many pets have been laid to rest complete with memorial headstones. Almost on the bridge itself is a Quakers' Meeting House built in 1715. This is a fascinating and little known building and inside is a chair once used by George Fox, the founder of the sect. The building has been little altered and the stables where the Friends, who had often travelled long distances to the services, kept their horses also still stand. In those far off days the meeting houses had to be situated in remote spots well away from possible persecution.

Crawshawbooth has one final claim to fame. Ask any east Lancastrian where the Devil played his football and you will be told either Turf Moor or Ewood Park depending whether the supporter comes from Burnley or Blackburn. Legend has it, however, that Old Nick last turned out for a game on one Sunday afternoon at Crawshawbooth. Apparently he played well until he kicked the ball so hard that it disappeared. When one of the lads noticed his cloven hooves and forked tail, Old Nick evaporated in a cloud of smoke and burning sulphur. These days they call it a free transfer!

 ## THE CROAL-IRWELL VALLEY

▬▬▬ No river system has been so ill-treated by industry as the Irwell. It was said not too long ago that if you fell into the Irwell you actually dissolved before you drowned. One of the Irwell's most polluted tributaries was the Croal and it is encouraging to see the efforts now being made to improve the water quality and therefore the wildlife which depends upon it.

Situated close to Farnworth's Hall Lane area is Rock Hall and this and the Crompton Lodges are both now integral parts of the Moses Gate Country Park. The Crompton family built both Vale House and Rock Hall which was completed in 1807. This is now the base of the ranger service and has an impressive small museum and a book shop.

The country park was once the base of the Farnworth Paper Mills owned by the Cromptons and in the early 19th century they still gave their address as near Bolton-Le-Moors. This is a sure sign that the Industrial Revolution had not yet begun in earnest and real pollution was still in its infancy. Bolton was only a small settlement in those days.

Robert Crompton had established a paper mill here during the mid 17th century and his descendants ruled the industrial roost for more than 200 years. They saw the Croal valley become more and more polluted as chemicals and bleaches were produced in connection with paper and textiles, and coal began to be mined.

Industry always needs water and as the Croal became ever more polluted and discoloured the Cromptons needed clean water for their paper. They built lodges to hold the water and to filter it. These have recently been cleaned and the areas around them landscaped to produce a magnificently wild habitat. Here are pochard, tufted duck, great crested grebe and large numbers of hungry looking mute swans and Canada geese.

The variety of wildlife is well described in the free leaflets which can be obtained from the Rock Hall centre where there is ample parking, and picnic and toilet facilities.

Despite its increasingly attractive museum and its environs Rock Hall is not usually listed in Lancashire's 'Places to visit'. It would be a pity if such an important part of Lancashire's history was to remain unpublicised.

CROSTON

——— Stone and brick-built cottages line one side of the village street, and on the other side the river Yarrow follows a twisting course between high and confining stone walls. The river is crossed by a narrow, arched stone packhorse span known as Town Bridge and bearing the date 1682. A set of alms-houses built by Henry and Isobel Croston in 1793 are also worth seeking out. These are not signed but are close to the church. The 16th century church of St Michael stands in the centre of the village, and is approached by a narrow street of brick cottages. At the entrance to the street stands a cross mounted on an ancient weatherworn plinth. Croston's Old English name means 'town of the Cross' and probably derives from a 7th century wayside cross where Celtic missionaries to northern England addressed worshippers before the church was built. The present crosshead, however, dates only from 1953, and was actually cut from an old mill stone. The base, however, is probably original.

On the opposite side of the church is the large white painted rectory, one of the finest Georgian buildings in the north of England and built by the De Trafford family. Next to the church is a school founded in 1372 by John of Gaunt, who was virtual ruler of England during the minority of Richard II. The school was given an endowment by the Puritan James Hyett, vicar of Croston, in 1660. Two years later Hyett was forced from the ministry for refusing to obey the Act of Uniformity which, among other demands unacceptable to a Puritan, included the use of the revised Anglican prayer book. Hyett died in Preston in 1663 and is remembered at Croston by a stone plaque on the school wall overlooking the churchyard.

There are far too few of Lancashire's old schools surviving and it is a pity that Croston's, one of the better examples, should not be as well known as the church, the cross and the rectory.

 ## CUERDALE

—— Known only by name by every Anglo-Saxon and Viking scholar in Britain because of the treasure of that period discovered there, Cuerdale receives few if any visitors because of the difficulty of access.

Near the parish church of Walton-le-Dale, on the outskirts of Preston, is Knot House. From here a footpath leads down to the river Ribble. Following the river downstream and just before Cuerdale Farm a small stone peeps out from among the reeds. It is inscribed 'Site of the Cuerdale Hoard, 15 May 1840' to indicate where the treasure was found by men working on the bank of the river. They must have been astounded to find that they had disturbed a lead box containing one of the richest treasures ever found in Britain.

Among the huge mass of ingots and richly ornate jewelry were about 7,000 coins all dated prior to AD 928 and minted in many different places including Mercia, East Anglia and even in France.

Young Queen Victoria, recently crowned, took a great interest in the coroner's inquest which ordered that the treasure should be distributed around the museums of the country. By then, however, some items had disappeared into the homes of the locals and it is rumoured that some are still part of the secrets of the original landowners' and workers' families.

Experts cannot agree on the precise reason for the existence of the hoard but most accept that a party of Vikings were on their way to reinforce the army of Anlaf in AD 937 when they were attacked by Saxons but managed to hide their war chest

The Victoria or Jubilee Tower, near Darwen.

before being slaughtered with none surviving and thus for 900 years the location of the treasure was lost.

DARWEN

Dominating the skyline above Darwen is the Victoria, also known as Jubilee Tower. Nobody can miss the structure but as it is not generally known that the tower is open few people take the trouble to climb the steps to enjoy the view. Darwen built its tower in 1897 to celebrate Queen Victoria's Diamond Jubilee. It stands proudly on top of a 1,225 ft hill, swept by wind but occasionally still and vibrant with the notes of lark and curlew. On the tower's viewing platform are plaques indicating the hills which can be seen in the distance; on a clear day you can see the Lakeland peaks, the Isle of Man, the Derbyshire dales, the Welsh mountains and of course the nearby glories of the Pennines.

The old Darwen mills are seen below in the valley once hidden by industrial smog, but these days most mills have closed and the air is clear. India mill is one of the most remarkable industrial buildings in Britain and its brick structure was designed in the style of the campanile situated in St Mark's Square in Venice.

The Lancashire textile industry was in full swing during the 1930s and India mill attracted an Indian statesman on a fact-finding mission. Ghandi came to Darwen in September 1931 and no doubt asked about the tower as all visitors do. Was he one of the few who climbed it to admire the view?

DEAN IN ROSSENDALE

In the old days anyone spending a night in one of the mill towns would be awakened first by the mill buzzers sounding a reveille, and this would be followed, before the second buzzer went, by a peculiar clattering which grew in volume until it was as though thousands of wooden hammers were beating on the pavement – the sound of wooden clogs. But, even at that time of the morning (and in winter it would be dark and probably raining) the sound would be mingled with laughter and singing.

A serpent – an instrument made by the Larks of Dean in the 18th century.

Music has long been a feature of the Lancashire moorlands and part of the county folklore is to be found in Rossendale especially around the village of Dean in the 18th century. The 'Deign Layrocks' or the Larks of Dean were well known as singers mainly of church music which they bought by each person chipping in a portion of their wages earned for the backbreaking work first at their handlooms sited in their hillside cottages and later in the mills which sprang up along the valley bottoms. First powered by water these were succeeded by steam powered mills built on the hills above the rivers. The Larks were often skilful enough to make their own instruments and a collection of these can be seen in the Whittaker Park Museum in Rawtenstall, among them a cello, a violin and a huge twisting monstrosity known as a serpent. Their music scores are also kept in the museum.

At the end of a long day's work the Larks would walk many miles to make music and would often rehearse until the early hours of the morning. They would pack up just in time to reach the mill for their next grinding shift with only the noise of the clattering looms to replace their own sweet music.

Dean village is situated just off the Burnley to Waterfoot road and high on the hills the farms and cottages once occupied by the former handloom weavers with the heavenly voices can still be seen. Some are now in ruins but many have been restored. How many are now occupied by members of the Rossendale Male Voice Choir which continues the traditions of the Layrocks right up to the present day?

DINCKLEY

—— Situated on the old road between Whalley and Ribchester is a sign indicating Dinckley. Follow the road through the village of splendid cottages to where a footpath descends steeply towards Dinckley Hall.

This substantial Tudor house is now a farmhouse and overlooks the river Ribble. A stile opens out to a couple of succulent green riverside meadows and leads to a footbridge. A plaque close by commemorates the opening of the bridge on 10th October 1951 by Sir Frederick Hindle, at that time the chairman of the Lancashire Highways and Bridges Committee. The bridge has been damaged several times by storms but this was a far better option for travellers than the rowing boat ferries which it replaced.

In days gone by this was an important trade route and the ferry service was vital. The origin of the term 'Trow Ferry' is interesting. It consisted of two hollowed out logs which were pulled on ropes from bank to bank. This ancient form of ferry was replaced from about the mid-19th century by a more traditional rowing boat which had to be summoned from Dinckley Hall, then leased as a farm which included the ferry concession. Those wishing to cross had to hail the farm until the ferryman responded. He was apparently deaf until he could see that the boat was full.

DOWNHAM

Downham is one of Lancashire's best known tourist traps and yet still maintained as an estate village governed from its Hall. Downham, set on the Roman road between Ribchester and Ilkley, would seem on the face of it to have nothing new to excite the tourist.

Go on a Sunday morning, however, sit on the seat near the gnarled old sycamore tree hanging over the stocks and listen to the church bells. Three of these called the monks of Whalley Abbey to prayer prior to its dissolution in 1536. Inside the church is a 16th-century font given by Whalley's last abbot John Paslew.

There can be few more attractive places to listen to the call of ancient bells than Downham, snuggled into the foothills of Pendle.

DUNSOP BRIDGE

Dunsop Bridge has long provided travellers through the Trough of Bowland with a fine ice-cream shop, conveniences and a charming green overlooking the river Dunsop. Children paddle, dogs chase sticks, most people picnic and a few use the modern telephone kiosk without realising its significance. British Telecom have celebrated the fact that this was the 100,000th of the new style kiosks to be erected. This event is documented by glass etchings on the box itself and also on wooden posts set into the ground around it. The points of the compass and of local interest are also indicated.

I have always been among the first to complain at the loss of the solid and beloved old red boxes, but here at Dunsop Bridge between Clitheroe and Lancaster is a new fangled box which in time will have its supporters fighting to preserve it as an historic monument.

 ## EAGLAND HILL

Many of the Fylde villages have long and well documented histories which serve to attract interested visitors. A look at the Ordnance Survey map, however, will reveal tiny hamlets often overlooked and most having a unique charm.

Between Garstang and Pilling is a sign to the right indicating a cul-de-sac leading to Eagland Hill. To the right is a pretty red brick church with its associated hall and set in a wall is a red postbox inscribed with the initials VR. There are not many of these red treasures left to remind us of the golden age of Victoria when the penny post which began in 1840 was in its infancy.

Another reminder of a bygone age is a set of swing-boats, all brightly painted and glinting in the sunlight. No doubt the boats are well used by the children from the numerous farms which surround the hamlet and which are also served by the attractive church. This is dedicated to St Mark but is controlled from the parish church of St John the Baptist at Pilling.

EDISFORD

Set on the banks of the river Ribble, Edisford has a picnic site, a caravan complex, and a swimming pool overlooked by a large car park from which leads a network of well used footpaths.

Why then in a book exploring the little known nooks and crannies of Lancashire has one of the busiest beauty spots in the county been included? A preacher was once taken to task because his sermons were too long. 'Thou woud'st not complain at what I put in,' he replied 'if only tha' knew what I'd missed out'. Edisford Bridge has therefore been included not because of what visitors see, but because of what they miss seeing.

Long before the bridge was built this was an important river crossing used by the Saxons – Edis-ford. The old ford can still be seen downstream of the bridge and was the site of an important and bloody battle. This was in 1137 when a strong Norman force sallied forth from Clitheroe Castle only to be slaughtered by a band of invading Scots who caught them crossing the river and hacked them to pieces. At this time it is thought that a leper hospital stood on the bank and perhaps on the site occupied by the Edisford Bridge Hotel opposite to the pleasure centre. All traces have long since gone but there are stones incorporated into a nearby farmhouse which may well have come from the leper hospital.

The disease caused by the bacillus *Mycobacterium leprae*, results in painful skin eruptions. It is usually confined to warmer climates and may well have been brought back from the crusades. Legend has it that a member of the De Lacy family who owned Clitheroe castle returned from the Holy Land with leprosy and it could well have been he who established the hospital.

EXTWISTLE HALL

——— Extwistle is a ruined hall on a minor road between Nelson and Worsthorne surrounded by a derelict farm. Usually the only creatures to view this architectural treasure are sheep and cows. Despite plans in 1979 to repair the building nothing happened.

By 1991 even more of the structure had fallen down. The hall was then set to become the centre-piece of a 150 room hotel complete with swimming pool and an 18 hole golf course. Again nothing happened, then or since. But oh yes it has. More of the roof has fallen down and the walls are bulging at an even crazier angle.

There has been a settlement on Extwistle Moor since Neolithic times (New Stone Age some 2,500 years ago). In 1190 the region was given by William the Conqueror to his follower Richard Malbisse who divided the manor of Extwistle in two and gave half to the Abbey of Newbo and the other half to a chap called Adam of Preston. By the year 1277 the Adams

Extwistle Hall.

family had given their share to the Cistercian Abbey of Kirkstall near Leeds.

Following the dissolution of the abbeys the estate was sold and in 1580 the magnificent Elizabethan Hall was constructed and by 1637 several impressive extensions and barns had been added.

Extwistle was never a major influence in the area such as Towneley or Gawthorpe but it is still far too important to be allowed to crumble away. These days it looks so much like a ghost house that it could well be given back to the original Adams family!

Will the next news be of a demolition order, even though a sensible and relatively inexpensive restoration programme is all that is required to rescue this potential jewel in Lancashire's crown?

FAIRFIELD

Situated on the outskirts of Manchester is Fairfield village built in 1785 to provide a place 'where Moravians might live and follow their own private avocations'. Their faith did not allow them to mix and thus the settlement has preserved a unique religious community of the late 18th century.

The Moravian church was founded by the followers of John Hus in 1457 and originated in Bohemia. The Moravians sent several hardworking missionaries to England from 1732 onwards and they played a vital role in the Evangelical movement which developed at this time.

Moravian communities were largely self-governing and planned their lives firstly around their church whilst their work was largely agricultural. The women, however, were famous for their embroidery skills and they built up a substantial trade.

The peace of Fairfield which is now preserved as a conservation area can best be appreciated by standing in front of the simple Scandinavian style church and marvelling at the skill used to dovetail the dwellings of the 'Sisters' and 'Brethren' into this formal plan.

The sexes were carefully segregated here with the unmarried 'sisters' living on one side and working in the laundry whilst the 'brethren' lived on the other and did the hard labour essential to keep the settlement running smoothly. Even the graves in the churchyard were sexually segregated.

Peace and tranquillity were there from the beginning. The surprise comes in the realisation that both these qualities have been retained whilst the little village of Manchester which was once just as peaceful has expanded outwards and become a major noisy industrial and commercial centre.

FENISCOWLES

On the road from Blackburn to Bolton and Chorley is the one-time village of Feniscowles, now a suburb of Blackburn. A number of mills were once powered here by the crystal clear waters of the river Darwen. Then came the Industrial Revolution and a number of steam powered paper mills named after the sun and the stars. In 1995 the area became a housing estate and is now looking pretty again as mills have closed and the river pollution improved.

In the dip of the road look for the gates of the now ruined Pleasington Hall. This was built for the Feilden family in 1808 and it was surrounded by a large deer park. Eventually the river Darwen became so badly polluted that the family felt obliged to move and added insult to injury by choosing to live at Scarborough in Yorkshire!

After the Feildens left the hall its gardens became pleasure grounds and remnants of this complex can still be seen by those who park away from the busy main road and take the trouble to explore the old estate.

Feniscowles Gardens were particularly popular during the First World War and many locals still remember it in the 1930s when the place generated affection. Those in search of happy times seem hardly to have noticed the polluted river. At the present time enough remains to enable the visitor to appreciate the attractions of this wonderful old hall abandoned during the days when muck and brass went hand in hand and cared not a jot for the environment. The area is now a haven for wildlife and Feniscowles is only hidden to those who are too shy to walk through the gates of the ruined hall and search out its nostalgia.

FLEETWOOD

Fleetwood has something of an identity crisis – is it a commercial port, a seaside resort or a fishing complex? At one time the point of balance was difficult to detect but now there is no doubt that its emphasis must be on tourism.

Such a major fishing port, however, must preserve its history and in 1987 a memorial was erected on the seafront near the North Euston Hotel. Dedicated to the hundreds of deep sea fishermen who sailed from Fleetwood and did not return it is fashioned in the form of a trawler gallows, which was the gear used to raise the heavy net full of fish from the water. Commemorated here is the loss of 42 ships and more than 400 men but the counting only began in 1900.

The memorial was unveiled by the mayor of Wyre – Antoon Vink. This was an ideal choice because Antoon had escaped in his trawler from his native Holland when the Germans invaded and made his home in Fleetwood. The memorial is as yet unknown because for some reason modern monuments, like good wine, take time to 'mature'.

When the history of Britain's tourist industry in the 1980s comes to be written, high on the list must be a heavy, almost fanatical concentration on steam locomotion.

Are there still steam engines lying about, becoming more and more rusty and hidden behind tangles of vegetation? Indeed there are and a large steam graveyard is situated close to Fleetwood docks.

This area is bound to bring a feeling of nostalgia as rusting hulks of old fishing trawlers rock to the rhythm of the tide in the docks whilst on the landward side of the quay are old engines perched on railway tracks. These mostly have been ripped up for scrap, leaving only those lines actually supporting a locomotive.

Until it was demolished this railway complex served the coal burning Fleetwood power station, the site of which is now literally reduced to rubble. Botanists love this place where bramble, mullein, ragwort, foxglove and biting stonecrop are particularly prominent.

It is, however, these forgotten kings of steam which make this area unique. These days if the wind is in the right direction the dominant aroma comes not from steam and coal

but from the nearby Fisherman's Friend lozenge factory which is based nearby.

John Lofthouse, a chemist, invented a liquid which was a proof against cold winds encountered by fishermen at sea. He mixed liquorice, capsicum, eucalyptus and menthol. Bottles do not survive rough weather and Lofthouse, whose descendants still own the company, soaked the liquid into a powder which when allowed to set is easy to transport. These were indeed Fisherman's Friends.

FOODEN HALL

In 1906 Fooden Hall was one of the best known houses in the Ribble Valley but is now very difficult to find. It is signed to the right just off the narrow winding road between Bolton-by-Bowland and Gisburn.

Once known as Stinking Farm, Fooden is a real gem and a reminder of the time before the National Health Service! The

Fooden Hall – once known as Stinking Farm.

house dates to the early 17th century but its glory days were during the late 19th century when it became a small but locally famous spa.

Water bubbles from a spring beneath a ledge of rock and as it flows it leaves a deposit of sulphur along its course alongside the hall. The smell of hydrogen sulphide, better known as rotten egg gas, is the first thing you notice but it has always been accepted in quack medicine that the more unpleasant the treatment the more effective is its cure.

Whilst searching out the almost forgotten history of Fooden I met Mrs Ruth Collinson whose maiden name was Wolfenden and who spent her childhood at the hall. Her father had great confidence in the quality of his spring and quoted the case of one of his favourite horses which always chose to drink the 'stinking water' in preference to the ordinary. As the mare produced 13 healthy foals in 13 years Mr Wolfenden assumed that his well had fertility properties.

Mrs Collinson said that her dad drank the water himself and that she had six brothers and two sisters.

'Nobody remembers the house or the spring much these days,' she said. 'Will you be putting it in your book?' How could I refuse?

FOULRIDGE

The Leeds to Liverpool canal, finally completed in 1816, is still open along the whole of its 127¼ mile length. The canal rises out of Yorkshire, through the Pennines across a flat plain and down into Lancashire before reaching the Mersey estuary at the Stanley Docks in Liverpool.

Foulridge is at the summit of the canal and the engineers had a financial problem to solve. Should they construct long staircases of locks to carry the canal up and over the summit or would it be cheaper to cut a tunnel through the hillside?

The latter was accepted as the best option and its construction was the greatest engineering feat of the late 18th and early 19th century and was the equivalent of our channel tunnel. In the early days boats were propelled through the tunnel by their crew pressing their feet against the walls, known as 'legging it', whilst the barge horses were led over the hills before rejoining their barges at the other end. Then came steam but now the traffic is diesel or petrol driven and controlled by lights on each side of the tunnel. In the last century a cow ignored convention by swimming through the tunnel and was rewarded by having its photograph on display in the bar of the Hole in the Wall public house in Foulridge.

Boaters know the pub and the tunnel well but many still find the mile long (actually just less than this) journey somewhat claustrophobic. Far too few landlubbers are attracted to this wonder of the canal age, many people who know Lancashire well think that the tunnel is closed. It is very much a working monument with a summer opening coffee shop and an underused car park close by.

There are several locks on either side of the tunnel and each time one is operated as many as 75,000 gallons of water are used. Compensation water had to be provided and reservoirs were built at Barrowford and at Foulridge. The latter is now a multi-purpose attraction with exclusive houses around it and facilities for anglers and boaters, but with parts sensibly set aside as a nature reserve. The reservoir still keeps the canal topped up although the cut only carries pleasure craft these days. Oh yes – there has been a name change. The locals no longer like to live at Foul-ridge and insist on calling the reservoir Lake Burwain! It must have been a foul-ridge for those navvies who were paid a pittance to hack their way through the tough Pennine rocks.

FRECKLETON

Until the flood plain of the Ribble was tamed by canalising the river, much of the land around Freckleton was marshy. Pushing roads through this terrain was always a problem but a fascinating insight into the turnpike roads of the Fylde can be seen between Halfpenny Bridge and Old Freckleton.

Just off the modern road from Preston to Lytham, a short track runs off through gates and towards the marshes. Here stands the old Toll House, now isolated but from it the line of the long grassed over turnpike road can be seen striking across the marshes.

The purpose of this road, built in the early 1800s, was to bring Lytham into closer touch with the developing business areas of Lancashire, then later it carried visitors to the new coastal resorts. In 1824 there were at least three coaches a day operating between Preston and Lytham.

The line of the old coach road can be seen even more clearly from the air. At a height of more than 4,000 feet in a hot air balloon I could see that the old road runs almost ruler straight across the marshes. Sweeping below, a flock of curlews' bubbling calls mingled surprisingly easily with the occasional rush of hot air from the burners and the creak of the basket as I moved around to get better views.

Apart from the sheer exhilaration of a hot air balloon flight one major advantage is quickly apparent. Many hidden areas are brought more sharply into focus, especially watercourses, long deserted villages and old roads.

✿ THE FYLDE MUSEUM OF COUNTRY LIFE

——— This museum is well worth a visit even though it is off the main tourist route. It is signed off the A6 road close to Garstang, a distance of about eight miles.

If you want to see a clinical museum run by professionals then this is not what you are looking for. It is a collection of material gathered by a farming family who know how every-thing which they have collected once worked. They should do because they either used it themselves, or friends of their parents or grandparents had been the operators.

Here are displays of butter and cheese making, peat cutting, cobbling, blacksmithing, wheelwrighting, ploughing, printing and clogging. There is what may well be a unique collection of milk bottles from all over the county. The Pilling telephone exchange which operated until the 1970s has been brought here and re-assembled. There are exhibits relating to both world wars and a wood turner is often in residence demon-strating his skills. Sometimes local people dress up in the costume of the 1920s, 30s and 40s and explain how the various exhibits work.

There is a display of animal traps (and a man trap) all of which are thankfully now illegal but are still an important part of the history of the countryside.

The opening times are from 11am to 5pm during April on Sunday only and in May on Saturday and Sunday. In June on

Wednesday, Saturday and Sunday and in July, August and September daily except Monday and Friday. In October the museum is only open on Sunday.

At other times the museum will open for groups by arrangement and some local schools are now using the facilities as part of their curriculum. There is a car park, also toilets, a café serving home made refreshments and from time to time there are special events. The main attraction of this museum, based around a rather remote farm, is its lack of professional marketing. There is nowhere else in the county quite like it.

GALGATE

—— The Fylde and Over Wyre have made their mark on the history of windmills, agriculture and fishing. The area's impact on the innovations which fuelled the Industrial Revolution, however, is minimal, but there is one glorious exception – the Galgate Silk Mills. These days Macclesfield in Cheshire is thought of as the birthplace of silk spinning and weaving and few historians realise that the first purpose built mill of this type was at Galgate.

There are really three mills on the site beginning in 1792 and ending with the red brick mill complete with its high chimney, built in 1851. The complex is now used as an industrial trading estate with several garages, a marine engineers, also furniture, carpet, curtain and blind manufacturers plus a pleasant little café.

Some historians complain that these historic mills are not being used properly and should be the centre of a heritage centre, but they overlook the important fact that if such huge buildings had not been used they would long since have fallen down and disappeard altogether. On a slow stroll around the mills you can almost feel their original architects thinking. There is the dried up pool of the mill reservoir leading to a leet and the site of the waterwheel. There are skylights in the flat roofs of the first mills to allow light on to the looms, enabling the workers to make use of every second of daylight. The arrival of first gas and then electricity meant that mills could operate a shift system and use all of the 24 hours in the day.

High on a wall is a clock under which the mill manager

would have stood on the lookout for late comers and to ensure that nobody sneaked out early or for a crafty fag.

The old mills are built of stone, looking rather like large barns. These two developments are functional yet still architecturally impressive whilst the later red brick mill gives the feeling of strength and prosperity but is not quite so friendly.

The buildings of Galgate around the mills also have a feel of history about them. There are rows of mill cottages, managers' houses and the magnificent Ellel House, now a retirement home run by the Lancashire Social Services and situated opposite the old mill pond. Nearby is St John's Church, a 19th-century building, but seeming much older because of the way it slots easily into the village pattern. In Galgate we have a little piece of Britain's more gentle industrial history which is almost – but not quite – forgotten.

 ## GARSTANG

Garstang is an ancient town which developed because it commanded a vital crossing of the river Wyre.

It has more than its fair share of old coaching inns and tea shops and it was in one of the latter that I overheard two students expressing their surprise that such an important town never had a castle. Any doubts about whether Greenhalgh Castle warranted an entry in *Hidden Lancashire* were dispelled by this long remembered conversation.

For many years Garstang was under the feudal rule of the Greenhalgh family who backed the right side in one of the most significant battles in English history. They provided a strong presence on the side of Henry Tudor (the seventh) who defeated Richard Plantaganet (the third) at Bosworth in 1485, and were rewarded by grants of land and the permission to construct their own heavily fortified castle.

By 1490 the Greenhalghs had raised a fine castle with corner towers of up to 60 feet in height and overlooking a meander in the Wyre, having a clear view of the town of Garstang and its vitally important bridge.

During the next major conflict the family chose the wrong side. They backed king against Parliament and their fortress was one of the last of the Royalist strongholds in Lancashire to surrender to the Roundheads.

After the war ended Cromwell ordered the castle to be dismantled and the local farmers were not slow to make use of it as an unofficial quarry. Below what is left of the castle – a low tower and a pile of stones standing in a grassy knoll – is Castle Farm. This is a lovely building constructed in the late 17th century entirely of plagiarised stone. From the castle a footpath leads down into the town and it is impossible to resist turning round to snatch yet another view of the historic pile. From Garstang itself Greenhalgh castle is hardly visible and probably because it is not well signposted except via the footpath it is likely to remain in splendid isolation.

GATHURST

The idea of a country stroll around Wigan may come as a surprise to many. So also will Gathurst which is a fascinating slice of industrial archaeology cocooned in a time warp. Close to the M6 Gathurst is a hamlet set in the valley of the river Douglas near Wigan and through which passes the Leeds to Liverpool Canal.

The Navigation Inn close to a bridge over the canal is the best place to start and from it is a wonderful view along the cut which is crossed first by a railway bridge and then by a massive road bridge carrying the M6 on concrete pillars.

From Wigan the canal descends via a staircase of locks down to a plain and then through Burscough and on to its terminus at Liverpool. Although seldom acknowledged this was a magnificent feat of engineering especially in the context of the time. The scientific expertise during the late 18th and early 19th centuries was in its infancy; all the workers had was muscle!

About a mile along the towpath Gathurst Locks are still operative and overlooked by the keeper's cottage. In the days when the canal was a busy commercial enterprise horses were stabled here. The cobbled towpath leading down from the locks was laid to prevent the barge horses from slipping. All these buildings remain but can only be reached via a long stroll which is perhaps why so few people take the trouble to explore the area.

To cope with the large numbers of barges using the canal at Gathurst there is a double system of locks and an ingenious weir feeding water into them. Some locks take as much as 75,000 gallons of water each time they are operated and it often costs as much to store and deliver this water as it did to build the main line of the canal itself.

These days the canal only handles pleasure craft, but apart from the railway and motorway bridges nothing much has changed here for nearly two centuries. In summer swallows and swifts swoop over the water and in the hedgerows the flower list is impressive, including white dead-nettle, stitch-wort, lords and ladies and jack-by-the-hedge.

The Navigation Inn, which provides substantial bar snacks, is a history lesson in itself with lots of old photographs showing the canal when it was working. There are displays of the knots used by the bargees which gives a nautical feel to the place, a collection of natural history drawings, and fish found in the canal mounted in cabinets. It is good to see canalside inns such as the Navigation which have retained all of their character.

The name navigation is interesting; those who travelled on inland waterways were navigators just like those who sailed the seas. The men who dug the canals were also called naviga-tors and the word was shortened to navvies which still survives to describe a labourer.

Gathurst is in the middle of a long and well maintained towpath walk between Wigan and Burscough but there is a shorter stroll from Gathurst and Appley Bridge and return, with good parking at either end.

Gathurst is a canal settlement in a time warp but Appley has kept more in touch with the times. Its basin is well used by colourful long boats and the canalside cottages have been tastefully restored.

GAWTHORPE HALL

—— Despite being splendidly maintained by the National Trust, Gawthorpe, situated between Padiham and Burnley, is one of Lancashire's least publicised halls. It is now a national craft centre thanks to donations given by its last resident, the Hon Rachael Kay-Shuttleworth.

Gawthorpe began as a pele tower, a strong square structure built as a defence against the invading Scots of the 14th century. Around 1600 the Revd Lawrence Shuttleworth built his mansion based around the pele but it was Sir Charles Barry who gave the hall its true glory in a sensitive restoration. This was done around 1850 and Barry may well have honed his skills at Gawthorpe before going on to design the Houses of Parliament.

Around this time the house was inherited by Sir James Kay who married the Shuttleworth heiress and the two joined their names by means of a hyphen. My introduction to Gawthorpe was as a student teacher whose college of St Mark's in Chelsea was founded by Sir James Kay-Shuttleworth who almost single-handedly revamped the educational system in the 1870s. Sir James had many friends in the literary field including the Brontës and it is said that Charlotte caught a cold and died as a result of a visit to Gawthorpe.

The house, thanks to Sir Charles Barry, looks Jacobean and its neat gardens overlook the river Calder. This has not always been the case. Until 1860 Gawthorpe and the Calder lived quietly together but then coal mines grew up around the hall, making money for the Shuttleworths. The mines so polluted the river that the family decided to move its course away from the noxious stench. Once the mines closed and the river became cleaner the Calder was brought back to its original bed! The alternative course can still be seen beneath a blanket of damp undergrowth.

GLASSON

―――― With the demise of many east coast ports during the late 18th century wars with revolutionary France the safer west coast ports increased their business and in the case of Glasson quite dramatically. A dock had been taking shape, in the planning stage at least, as early as 1738. The foundation stone was laid in 1751, but work did not commence until 1783, to be finally completed in 1840, when Glasson had a magnificent dry dock.

During the early 19th century Glasson was increasing its trade to such an extent that a bottleneck developed, and this was alleviated by the construction of an arm connecting the port to the main line of the Lancaster Canal. This was completed by 1820.

A splendid walk leads from Glasson marina along the canal towpath and past the attractive little church of All Saints. This was consecrated in 1840 at a time when the port was expanding and it has some interesting stained glass, especially relating to the Starkie family. They lived at Ashton Hall which is now the 19th hole of Lancaster Golf Club.

Near the entrance gate and to the left of the church is a headstone commemorating the lives of the husband and wife team, Thomas and Marguerite Tiller who have nothing to do with the steering gear of boats but were the founders of the famous troupe of long-legged dancing girls. Thomas (1870-1946) and Lenore Marguerite (1878-1964) spent their lives literally in the spotlight but their ashes are here wrapped in a web of peace.

These days the only leggers of Glasson are the walkers who usually pass the church and the 'dancers' stone' without so much as a second glance.

GREAT HARWOOD

—— Situated roughly between Blackburn and Whalley, Great Harwood has a 15th-century church and an interesting clock dominating the town square.

'Its nobbut a clock,' replied a lady in her 90s who had worked as a weaver in the town for 80 years. She had been asked on a radio programme what she knew about the clock. Actually it is much more than a mere clock and celebrates the life of John Mercer. This quite remarkable man discovered how to make parchment paper but also how to 'mercerise' fabrics. The process increases the lustre of cotton fibres. It consists of treating the material with concentrated caustic soda, which causes swelling and, providing the material is kept under tension, also results in the fibres becoming transparent.

John Mercer was born in 1791 in the nearby hamlet of Dean. He was one of many Lancastrian inventors whose work in the field of textiles is now largely forgotten. At least he has fared better than most in having the process which he invented at Great Harwood named after him – and there is also his monument which is 'nobbut a clock'.

HALE

Is it possible to overlook a giant? Not the giant himself perhaps, but his grave can lie almost forgotten as is proved by a visit to the Merseyside village of Hale.

Only a stone's throw from Liverpool and dovetailed into the banks of the Mersey is this charming village of thatch. Still here in all its splendour is the village green and a twisting road leads down to the disused lighthouse which is now part of a residence – it looks like the world's tallest garden shed. This is the most southerly point of old Lancashire.

The splendid and ancient church is passed on the way to the lighthouse and in the cemetery lies the mortal remains of John Middleton, the 'Childe of Hale'. Some child this because he measured 9ft 3 inches. The thatched cottage in which he was born in 1578 still stands in the village although Hale Hall which he often visited to demonstrate his wrestling skills has been demolished. It can never be known how talented John was as a wrestler but his sheer size would have been quite enough to ensure fame.

He was taken to London and easily defeated the champion of King James I. The king by all accounts was not too pleased but still gave John Middleton £20 and a suit of clothes. On the way home the giant was feted at Brazenose College in Oxford, closely associated then as now with Lancashire scholars. His portrait can still be seen in the college and his walking stick has also been preserved there.

When he died in 1623 another portrait was made and this is a life-size and quite awe inspiring reminder of Lancashire's giant. It hangs in nearby Speke Hall which is situated alongside Liverpool airport and like Hale, close to the river Mersey.

HALTON

Now only a small village enfolded in the crooked arm of the Lune and overlooked by the bridge carrying the M6 over the river, Halton is a mere backwater.

This was not always the case and for a while it was a toss up whether Halton or nearby Lancaster would be the administrative centre of what later became Lancashire. The title of this book could just as well have become Hidden Haltonshire, and the quiet village described here would then have been Lancaster!

The Romans got Lancaster off to a dominant start by building their fort (caster) on the Lune, but once the Romans had gone their settlement declined. There may have been some Roman activity around Halton, however, because an altar, probably dedicated to Mithras their sun god, is now incorporated into a wall of the church. When these north lands came into the possession of Tostig, the brother of the ill-fated King Harold, he chose Halton as his administrative centre. Tostig built his hall (Halle) on top of the mound which now overlooks the church and carries a flagpole although all trace of the hall has gone.

It was at this Halle in 1065 that Tostig, after having been deposed as Earl of Northumbria, decided that he must oppose Harold. In 1066 the two brothers met in battle at Stamford Bridge near York. Tostig was killed and Harold was licking his wounds when the message reached him that the Normans were invading. After a long, fast and hard march south a tired Harold and his troops were defeated at Hastings, and Harold himself was killed. English history may well have been different if Tostig of Halton had decided to accept his brother as king and work with him. William would then have had to face two well-rested and strong armies instead of one, weakened and weary after a battle and a march.

In the churchyard below the old Halle site is a Norse preaching cross with pagan symbols on one side showing Sigurd at his forge, surrounded by the tools of a blacksmith, and Volsung. They seem to be roasting the heart of a serpent on a spit. The ascension of Christ is shown on the other side. This is another example of pagans accepting Christianity but still reluctant to reject their old gods just in case.

Following the Norman victory William first devastated the north and then gave Tostig's lands to Roger of Poitou who chose Lancaster as his base. Halton has been an unimportant village ever since. This is very much a story of what might have been ... if only.

HEALEY DELL

A tree-lined valley rich in flowers, Healey Dell nature reserve snuggles along and beneath an aqueduct towering 105 feet above the river Spodden. The 200 ft long, eight-arched viaduct was built around 1880 to carry the railway from Rochdale to Bacup. It is said that Lord Byron, who was lord of a manor near Oldham, visited Healey regularly in pursuit of a beautiful young lady.

The nature trail begins close to the main Bacup road, and follows the elevated railway line which provides spectacular views over and beyond the dell. The railway closed in the 1960s, but the haunting ruins of the old station at Broadley can still be found amid tangled vegetation. Below, the river Spodden tumbles through the narrow, winding dell with waterfalls and grottoes which legend tells us were also a haunt of Robin of Locksley who wooed a lass from Healey Hall. A few of the locals still stroll around Robin Hood's Well. It is said that he was almost snared by a witch and some of the stones in the well have been eroded by water into grotesque human-like shapes. This no doubt inspired the legend.

With such illustrious connections as Byron and Robin Hood it is difficult to understand how Healey Dell has managed to hang on to its lonely mysteries without becoming part of an established tourist trail.

HELMSHORE

The village of Helmshore stands astride a complex of mills which are now part of an excellent museum deserving more praise than it is usually given. The museum here is just as much a part of our heritage as a church, cathedral, castle or an area of outstanding countryside.

Helmshore did not exist until 1789 when the Turner family bought a number of fields in the parish of Musbury on the banks of the river Ogden which is a tributary of the Irwell. The family had cotton mills in Blackburn and woollen mills at Martholme near Rishton.

The Turners built a water powered woollen mill and then set out to attract workers and construct cottages for them to live in. The mill eventually converted to cotton. The old water wheel and lodges can still be seen snuggled below the old railway line which obviously came later. This line is now closed but had it been connected to the East Lancashire Steam

Railway they could have combined to produce a major tourist attraction.

In the 1820s a second mill was constructed and since this time the two mills have caused confusion. There are several reasons for this. Both mills became known as Higher Mill and then after the Turner family had run out of male heirs to oversee their business they were sold. One mill was bought by the Whitaker family (with one t) and the other by the Whittaker family (with two ts). Whittaker's (the older mill) closed in 1967, Whitaker's in 1978 and the mill and its machinery were then purchased by the Lancashire County Council who received grants from the Department of the Environment and the Science Museum. Following a period of hard work the museum opened in 1984. Wildlife is returning to the area and around the old lodge kingfisher, dipper and grey wagtail have all been regularly seen as have heron and mink.

Inside the museums is a treasure trove of the industrial machinery from the textile age. Here is the only working example of an Arkwright water frame to be found anywhere in the world. There is also a spinning jenny and the water wheel of the old mill still works as do a large proportion of the looms. The history of the textile industry is also explained in a number of old photographs.

The 'Higher Mill' complex was not the only enterprise evolved by the Turners. There was also the nearby Middle Mill and by the 1960s this was owned by Platt Brothers of Oldham who built textile machinery. In 1971 the Platt collection was moved to the Helmshore Mills on permanent loan, and this too is of world importance.

Helmshore Textile Museums are now used by schools with guided visits offered as part of the curriculum. This is understandable, but the surprising fact is that so many Lancashire people fail to appreciate its attractions. They have been told so often that they live among muck and chimneys and with no tourist attractions that they tend to believe this.

HEST BANK

Known to every serious birdwatcher in the North West of England the Royal Society for the Protection of Birds (RSPB) reserve at Hest Bank receives its fair share of visitors.

The salt marshes and sands beyond the railway station provide roosting and feeding grounds for many thousands of wading birds and wildfowl while predators such as hen harriers, short eared owls and the occasional peregrine arrive for the easy pickings. In the summer botanists also come to enjoy the salt marsh flowers such as thrift, sea aster, the delightful sea spurrey and tiny pearlwort.

Whilst its natural history now gives the village a high profile its history really is obscure. Hest Bank was once a vital stop on the dangerous coach route across the sands. With the coming of the railway the coaching business came to an abrupt halt but it is still possible with just a little patience and imagination to follow the coach road through the village.

First find the Hest Bank hotel which was at one time much more isolated and not hemmed in by modern buildings. Here is the old lantern turret which once beamed a light out over the sands to guide the coaches to a safe haven and the horses, coach crew and passengers to a warm meal and perhaps somewhere to sleep.

Look down from the hotel and imagine that the railway line between you and the shore did not exist. Cross the level crossing to the RSPB car park. Do not stop but follow the track beyond a group of cottages. The old coach road continues straight as an arrow until it disappears into the hard sands of Morecambe Bay.

You have just followed what was once one of Lancashire's most important roads but now only used by naturalists, the vast majority of whom do not even wonder why such a well made track exists here and apparently leads to nowhere.

 ## HEYSHAM

────── Modern Heysham is famous as a ferry terminal linking with Ireland and the Isle of Man and also has its share of controversy generated by the recently constructed nuclear power station. This has its own visitors' centre and nature trail.

Ancient Heysham was the cradle of north western Christianity. On the cliff-top above the village is the ruined chapel of St Patrick which is only 28 feet by 9 feet. It is the only surviving example of a Saxon single-cell chapel in England. Close by are several graves cut out of the solid rock with spaces cut for the head and a socket into which a wooden cross could be inserted. Obviously the graves would be covered by stone slabs but these have been lost.

St Peter's church, situated in a dip below the chapel, is often mistaken for St Patrick's and some visitors never progress beyond this delightful building especially in spring when it is surrounded by a carpet of crocuses or when a wind is spectacularly driving the tide into the bay below the churchyard.

It is within the church, however, that Heysham's most famous artefact is hidden – a very rare example of a complete hog's head tomb typical of a Viking chief. Until recently it was in the churchyard but when threatened by weather erosion the tomb was removed into the church. Being secreted away within the building has taken away some of the drama of the memorial, which may have covered the last resting place of Thorold the Viking. A wild man, beard blowing in the wind and at the helm of his long ship would have wished to be remembered by a tomb exposed to the elements which he had challenged all his adult life. The tomb has Christian symbols plus the representation of a bear chewing away at each end and runic symbols along the sides. It was probably carved in this way at the bidding of the Viking who, although converted to Christianity, still thought it prudent to hedge his bets just in case the gods of his fathers held the keys to Heaven – or was it Valhalla?

 ## HODDER BRIDGES

—— Those who love crystal clear rivers and graceful spans should add the Hodder bridges to their list of places to visit. Between Whalley and Hurst Green the traveller can enjoy two bridges for the price of one with the older of the two hidden away downstream of the more modern span which was built as part of the turnpike road of 1826.

The old packhorse bridge, built in 1512, is usually referred to as Cromwell's Bridge and after a period of neglect has recently been restored. Oliver Cromwell certainly crossed over the bridge on his way to the battle of Preston in 1648. Some fanciful reports suggest that the Parliamentary army also tramped over the bridge, but close examination of the hump backed span show it to be far too narrow for this ever to have been considered. Good generals never attempt the impossible! Following a footpath which is almost swamped beneath a tangle of vegetation leads down to the old ford close to the 1512 bridge, so a much more reasonable suggestion is that Cromwell held a council of war close to the bridge to discuss how his heavy ordnance, especially cannon, powder and shot could be kept dry whilst being pulled over the ford.

The flat stones of the old ford are still there and in the clear water swirling around them numerous brown trout and the occasional salmon can be seen, making the Hodder a popular river with anglers.

HOGHTON

A drive leading up to Hoghton tower passes close to a substantial gatehouse. This is set on the A675 Blackburn to Preston road where stands an impressive war memorial. The tower is one of the most interesting houses in Britain. It is open on bank holidays and Sundays throughout summer and also on Saturdays during July and August. The drive which is lined with rhododendrons is an absolute treat during the late spring and early summer. Despite its obvious attractions Hoghton tower is usually not listed as one of Lancashire's main halls. It ought to be in the top six!

The tower is the home of the de Hoghton family who came over with William the Conqueror and their dwelling must have been impregnable at one time. The present structure dates mainly to the 16th century, and stands proudly on a hill overlooking the river Darwen. It is constructed around two courtyards, the first entered from the drive and through a gatehouse tower guarding a terrace and a rose garden which delights summer visitors, and is kept as a reminder of Old England.

Inside there is a collection of antique dolls and dolls' houses, but the tower itself has some magnificent rooms including the famous banqueting hall. It was here in 1617 that James I was entertained and was so impressed with a bit of loin beef that he knighted it and thus we have the sirloin. This event is also commemorated in the name of the local pub. The table at which the king tucked into his juicy steak is said to be still in its original position.

A pleasant walk follows an obvious track which goes round the back of the lodge and alongside an area of fine mixed woodland in which are found grey squirrels and a variety of birds.

HOLLINGWORTH LAKE

—— Hollingworth Lake is a Country Park overlooked by the M62. It is situated between Rochdale and Littleborough. There is a well appointed visitors' centre with toilets, book shop, café and information centre, and good facilities for children and for the disabled. A wheelchair is available for hire at the centre. Considering its attractions it is difficult to understand why it does not receive more visitors.

Hollingworth is not a natural lake but a compensation reservoir of 120 acres constructed to supply the Rochdale Canal with water; it opened in 1804 to link Sowerby Bridge with Manchester. At the present time it still supplies the surrounding area of canal with up to two million gallons a day, in addition to having a central role within the country park. The stretch of water was, however, popular with the hard-working mill hands in Victorian times who used it as a 'lung' situated high above the smoky town of Rochdale. The country park was opened in 1974 and since that time has gone from strength to strength. The visitors' centre features an excellent taped slide show giving details of the history and natural history of the area, but anyone with a couple of hours to spare and the stamina to cover 2½ miles will find the circular nature trail a real treat.

From the area of Hollingworth, the bulk of Blackstone Edge can be seen rising to a height of around 1,550 feet above sea level, over which runs a Roman road, much of it still in an excellent state of repair. Close to the lake is the Fish Inn and by the lake are several marshy areas in which grows water mint, yellow iris, water forget-me-not and ragged robin.

The footpath follows the line of an old road, and approaches a one-time toll gate close to which is a metal sign which has been restored and provides a feeling of history. This is particularly the case as you approach the hamlet of Hollingworth Fold, which must have been even more isolated before the reservoir was built. In the 19th century it had a workhouse, a small school and its own public house called the Mermaid. Perhaps it was anticipating the coming of the lake!

The nature trail then earns its name by entering an area of marshland which provides a refuge for a wide variety of birds, insects and plants. Here are found breeding great crested grebes, coot, snipe and mallard. The trail then reaches an area known as the promontory which in Victorian times was known as 'Weavers' Seaport', an attractive name inspired by the mill-hands who found clean air and relaxation here. When viewed in May and June with rhododendron at its best it is really beautiful. The Victorians certainly knew how to enjoy themselves and a paddle steamer which operated on the lake was often full to overflowing during the warmer months. Fortunately we can still enjoy a short trip on the *Lady Alice*, a motor cruiser.

Surely no country park can offer such variety as Hollingworth. The 'Weavers' Seaport' has still not lost its nautical air and yet careful and sensible management has resulted in an area very rich in wildlife, a feature which is becoming more obvious as the years go by – a perfect balance between leisure, history and natural history. But Hollingworth's assets are certainly not fully appreciated either by residents or especially by visitors to the county.

HOLLINSHEAD

Situated along the Roddlesworth Nature Trail between Blackburn and Darwen is Hollinshead Hall. It is now a ruin but archaeologists have been working for some years and have excavated the layout of the original buildings.

In the 1980s North West Water had to take action to prevent stone being removed and sold to garden centres in the London area. If this protective action had not been taken all signs of Hollinshead would have vanished.

Medieval documents mention the hall and whilst the building itself could never be rated as a major stately home, Hollinshead was an important centre for pilgrimages. Its fame was dependent upon the existence of the Well House where water still flows from a fountain depicting a beautifully carved lion's head. The water then flows into a series of troughs, and vast quantities were dispensed in the days when pilgrims thought that it cured eye complaints. Certainly the water is pure and in medieval times when hygiene was not a priority the ritual use of unpolluted wells as a place to treat many ailments almost certainly worked.

Hollinshead Well House still survives as does the fountain and troughs. Its fame has faded and on my last six visits I saw nobody at all – making the Well House surely the best kept secret in the county.

 ## HORNBY

────── Hornby is situated close to the confluence of the river Wenning with the river Lune and was settled long before the Norman Conquest. The castle, which overlooks the Wenning and the bridge across it, is a solid structure and like the church is forever associated with the battle of Flodden of 1513 at which the English routed the Scots. Edward Stanley was created Lord Monteagle by the grateful Henry VIII on that day, and as his personal war memorial the new lord added a splendid octagonal tower to St Margaret's church.

Hornby Castle, however, existed long before Flodden and although the bulk of the present structure is Georgian and Victorian all the additions surround an ancient pele tower of enormous strength built as a defence against the Scots during the 14th century.

Surprisingly, despite its history Hornby is not regarded as a major Luneside tourist attraction but remains largely unknown. Even those who know and love the castle and the church miss the assortment of Saxon crosses in the churchyard. Kept safely inside the church is another cross which is thought to be unique in England. It is carved with loaves and fishes and may once have had a wheel-shaped top section. The remnants of several other crosses and grave slabs came from Hornby Priory which was dissolved in 1537.

Lord Monteagle was buried at the Priory but all traces of this have long vanished and even the location of the last resting place of one of England's greatest warriors has been lost. Whether eagles ever soared above the castle mound is not known, but Hornby had its own formidable predator – the Stanley who earned the title of Monteagle from Henry VIII himself.

HURST GREEN

Apart from the modern cars parked outside the Shireburn Arms Hotel the scene at Hurst Green has changed little since the 1950s. During term time the village is often full of boys who attend Stonyhurst College one of the foremost Roman Catholic public schools in Britain. The school was once the stately home of the Shireburn family although the spelling of the name varies a great deal and has long been the subject of historical debate.

The 17th century Shireburn alms-houses between the village and the school are usually ignored by visitors but have a most fascinating history. They are reached by a flight of steps screened by balustrades and look to have been settled on the present site for centuries. They were, however, built in 1706 and situated on the nearby hill of Kemple End. By the 1940s they were derelict, and were purchased by the college, moved stone by stone and rebuilt in the village to serve as houses for its employees.

A slightly inclined road bordered on either side by conifers which provide cover for deer, sparrowhawk, owl and pheasant, leads out of the village. A sudden right turn leads into an avenue at the end of which stands Stonyhurst school in all its glory.

Stonyhurst as a college has been a roaring success, but as a family house it was a disaster. In 1702 when the fine new mansion was in the process of construction the young son and only male heir of Sir Nicholas died poisoned, so it is said, by eating yew berries. The family lost interest in the building and when Sir Nicholas Shireburn himself died the house was inherited by his daughter who was married to the Duke of Norfolk. On her death the house passed to the Weld family; they leased it to the Jesuits who moved their school from France to this glorious setting.

During the holidays the school opens to the public; its library is one of the finest in England and includes the prayer book which Mary Queen of Scots held in her hand as she was executed.

Stonyhurst school is well known to many Lancastrians but few know that the library is sometimes open, or are aware of the fascinating travels of the alms-houses.

HURSTWOOD

Situated in the valley of the river Brun just off the Burnley to Todmorden road lies the historic hamlet of Hurstwood. Its history might well go back beyond the year AD 937 when the battle of Brunenburk was fought. It is only fair to point out that other areas of Britain also claim to be on the site of this possibly legendary battle, but Hurstwood does at least have a 'battle stone' set in a secluded spot down by the riverside. The village, with its 16th-century hall, may well have been familiar to Edmund Spenser, author of *The Faerie Queene*, *The Shepeardes Calender* and other poems which delighted the first Queen Elizabeth.

> And just beside these trickled softly downe
> A gentle streme whose murmuring wave did play
> Amongst the punny stones, and made a sowne
> To lull him fast asleep that by it lay

There is no doubt that Spenser's house, which still stands and once smothered by ivy, belonged to relatives of the poet,

Spenser's Cottage.

and a great deal of indirect evidence can be gleaned from his writings which contain a large number of dialect words well known in this area. This is particularly noticeable in *The Shepeardes Calender* and, in a letter to Gabriel Harvey, Spenser himself mentioned his use of dialect. He could hardly have picked these up without long contact with his northern relatives.

> The gentle shepherd sat beside a spring
> All in the shadow of a bushy brere

This quotation from Spenser could almost have been written in the 'Lanky twang' of a modern dialect poet. He seems to have fallen in love with a northern lass – probably Rose Dyneley, a relative of the Towneleys – who preferred another suitor. The spirit of Rose seems to enter into the fabric of *The Faerie Queene* and it may well be that the poet's thoughts frequently returned to the lass and to the leafy glades around Hurstwood.

Neither is it any wonder that Spenser showed such an intimate knowledge of plants demonstrated in *The Shepeardes Calender* if he spent part of his youth in this still idyllic but little known spot.

 ## HUYTON

> Huyton, Huyton,
> Two dogs fightun,
> One's a black and
> One's a white un

This poem, or should it be referred to as doggerel, takes us back to the days when Huyton was infamous for its dog fights. It has in recent years only been famous as part of the parliamentary constituency of Prime Minister Harold Wilson during the 1960s and 70s.

Only six miles from the centre of Liverpool, Huyton village has been almost but not quite swamped by the expanding city. The parish church is dedicated to St Michael and although the present building is mainly 12th century there was a Saxon settlement on the site.

In 1873 extensive repairs being carried out to St Michael's uncovered some fascinating objects including the capitol from a Saxon column on which was carved four helmeted heads. The same workmen also discovered two so-called Nuremberg tokens which were similar to some found on the site of Birkenhead Priory across the Mersey. These were used throughout the Middle Ages as monastic dole tokens which could be exchanged for food and other essential materials.

Huyton would be of great interest if only for this find but it also has the doorway of the old village gaol embedded in the churchyard wall. There seems to have been what almost amounts to a fetish hereabouts for incorporating history into walls. At the back of the council offices, stone railway sleepers complete with a plaque are embedded in the wall. On the outside of the station are more of these sleepers, which were originally part of George Stephenson's railway line between Manchester and Liverpool. In 1830 the famous *Rocket* rattled over these structures.

During those far off days Huyton was set in green fields and it is still possible to appreciate this long vanished situation by standing on the village green and looking at the old market cross. This feeling of peace can be spoiled by the thought of dogs and cocks 'fightun' and bulls being baited which were all once widespread 'sports' hereabouts.

INCE BLUNDELL

The name of this village, situated to the south-east of Formby, is shrouded in some mystery. Ince is thought to derive from the Celtic word Ynes meaning an island, and so it must have been until drainage schemes brought more land under the plough. Once postal services evolved some confusion arose with the larger settlement of Ince near Wigan and so Blundell was added to its name.

If you fancy an odd collection of forgotten follies then Ince Blundell Hall is the place to go. It was built in 1778 by Henry Blundell who had become dissatisfied with his Tudor half-timbered Hall. Perhaps his desire for change came because of his travels on the continent during which he made impressive collections of classical art.

The hall is now a convalescent home but Henry Blundell's follies can still be seen although it is probably doing the man a disservice by not accepting the embellishments to his house as works of art in their own right. Take the so-called Pantheon for example. It now looks out of place and attached like a dislocated limb on the far side of the mansion, but it was purpose built to house Henry's vast collection of paintings and drawings. It only looks grotesque when stripped of these assets. The same applies to the Garden Temple, built to provide the right setting for a collection of Greek and Roman statues, and also to the Lion Gate. This stands at the entrance to the hall, and close by is the Priests' House which is of a strange shape with flattened sides but in the form of a circle and even its chimneys are circular.

Ince Blundell Hall also has a tradition thought to have been introduced from Belgium almost a century ago. Holy Family church which is associated with the hall has an annual ceremony during which the gravestones are decorated with flowers, lit by candles and are used as part of a torchlight procession, ending with a service.

KERSAL

—— Kersal, now a mere suburb of Manchester, on a meander of the river Irwell, snuggles below a hill which was once an important Iron Age settlement. The most prominent building is the rambling black and white Kersal Cell, the ancestral home of the Byroms. It stands on the site of a priory cell dating back to early Norman times.

> God bless the King, I mean the faith's defender,
> God bless (no harm in blessing) the Pretender
> But who Pretender is or who is King,
> God bless us all! thats quite another thing.

This amusing poem written by John Byrom who lived at Kersal Cell stresses the confusion all too evident at the time of the Jacobite rebellion of 1745. Byrom also deserves fame for his development of a patented system of shorthand. His enduring fame, however, derives from his writing of the hymn tune 'Christians Awake' which he first read out loud to his daughter on Christmas morning 1745.

Manchester Cathedral has its Byrom chapel where John was buried in 1763. There is a record of his family being fined £5 because his body was not wrapped in wool. This law had applied from medieval times to ensure a ready sale for wool with the Crown gathering in a very handy tax.

KNOWLE GREEN

This hamlet was once on the Roman road out of Bremettenacum Fort which is known today as Ribchester. The road then led to a second but much smaller fort at Overbarrow on the river Lune. Most of the Roman road now lies beneath the modern road linking Whalley and Longridge. A footpath leads off the main road to Dilworth House Farm and then to the mysterious Written Stone next to a farm of the same name.

If you enjoy being on your own and also being confused by history then this is the ideal place. Nobody seems to know why the stone was so inscribed. It is 11 ft long, 18 inches wide and bears an inscription which is now just legible telling us that 'Ravffe Radcliffe Laid this stone to Lye Forever 1655'. It is still there but its origins are obscure, making the Written Stone one of Lancashire's greatest mysteries.

If you believe in ghosts then you should avoid visiting the stone at night because some say that this is 'boggart' country. The Radcliffes had their reasons for leaving this particular stone unturned but these did not impress a family who lived there later. Several horses and sweating men were needed to shift the stone but after this the boggart created havoc in the area with horses regularly being 'spooked' into throwing off their riders. It was decided to return the Written Stone to its original position. This time it took just one horse and one man to do the job, but perhaps the boggart itself was helping. Peace was immediately restored.

LANCASTER

Everyone in the county knows of Lancaster Castle mainly because of its use as a court and as a prison. Not all know that its historic areas are open to the public and the guided tours are particularly informative.

Few people, however, know of the existence of Horseshoe Corner. Here set in the roadway is a replica of a shoe cast by the horse of John of Gaunt in the 14th century. It is set into the surface of the roadway close to the castle.

Look out also for the Conservative Club, a delightful Georgian house where Bonnie Prince Charlie stayed during the Jacobite rising of 1745.

Set close to the busy main street is the entrance to Penny's Almshouses constructed in 1720 by a local benefactor. It seems to be as tranquil and undisturbed today as it was when the first coat of blue paint was brushed around the polished brass door knockers. Penny's gift continues almost unheard of amid the rumble of traffic and the nearby Bashful Alley is also overlooked in the bustle.

The city is always full of visitors but few notice a cast shoe, a defeated pretender, and one who spared much more than a penny!

 ## LATHOM

—— Once one of England's greatest stately homes, Lathom Hall has vanished, a victim of the Civil Wars of the 1640s.

Whilst the seventh Earl, Lord Derby was away either fighting for King Charles or seeking refuge in the Isle of Man his countess, the redoubtable Charlotte de la Tremouille, was left at home. She took her duties seriously and really did 'hold the fort'. Charlotte marshalled her 300 man troop so well that they resisted the Parliamentary siege of 1644, losing only six men to the reputed 600 lost by the Roundheads. This proves how strong the Lathom battlements were.

The following year, however, the Parliamentarians returned and this time they were better organised and more patient, prepared to starve the countess out. Eventually when the king's cause was obviously lost Charlotte surrendered. Eager to avenge their troops lost the previous year Parliament ordered the magnificent Stanley mansion to be totally demolished.

Although a new and less spectacular building was erected in the 1720s this was also demolished in 1920. The site on which it stood is now occupied by Pilkington's Research and Development Laboratories. Nearby is a museum covering the history of glass making through the ages.

Many books record the sad demise of the hall but there is little mention of one surviving reminder of the Derby's grand home – Lathom Park chapel.

Dedicated to St John the Divine this is situated close to the laboratories and was founded in 1500 by the Second Earl of Derby. A set of 18th-century alms-houses has been built nearby without adversely affecting the attraction of the chapel.

During the two civil war sieges the Roundheads apparently acted with more sensitivity than was usual in these sad times. General Egerton seems to have kept his men in order and the plain but atmospheric interior was largely spared. He could not, however, prevent some soldiers from using the interior as a stable or letting off the odd musket at the 'Papist furniture'. Despite these acts of vandalism Egerton without question deserves the credit for saving the chapel.

The chapel has been restored several times in recent years but none of these have destroyed its character either. The chancel screen and eagle lectern were both brought from Burscough Priory following its dissolution. I once talked to a tour guide who knew that Lathom Chapel existed but thought that it was but an empty shell which had not recovered from the loss of the wonderful house which it once served.

Lathom was perhaps Lancashire's greatest medieval house and yet many people are unaware of this one tiny remnant of its glory which now remains to us.

LEA

——— Lea (pronounced Lee-ar) is a village totally swamped by the expanding conurbation of Preston. The name has not changed since Domesday which actually lists two settlements – French Lea and English Lea belonging to the de Hoghtons. The two were divided by Savick Brook, a tributary of the Ribble.

Approaching Preston from Blackpool on the A583 a bridge designed for farm animals crosses the road and just to the right is Old Hall Farm. This was a de Hoghton manor house – its half timbering now smothered beneath stone and brick cladding.

The building is a thriving farm but it may well have literary connections of the highest pedigree. Many historians believe that 17 year old Will Shakeshaft performed at the Old Hall and was part of Thomas Hoghton's travelling band of singing boys. We know Will Shakeshaft better as William Shakespeare and he is also said to have performed at the main de Hoghton manor at Rufford Old Hall on the road between Liverpool and Preston. This is now a National Trust house which gets all the Shakespearian publicity leaving Old Hall Farm at Lea as a forgotten house. I almost but not quite resisted the temptation to refer to King Lea!

During the 16th and 17th centuries Lea Old Hall was a haven for Catholic priests on the run from their fierce Protestant persecutors. Surrounded by neat hedges and very difficult of access, Lea Old Hall has lost all trace of this strife and looks just the place to have once inspired a budding playwright.

 ## LEYLAND

—— Leyland is world famous to those interested in the history of public transport, especially buses and lorries. This, plus the presence of a huge ordnance factory may suggest that the town is the product only of the 20th century. The best way of correcting this error is to pay a visit to the underrated Heritage Museum, formerly the old grammar school which was saved from demolition when threatened by a proposed construction of a town centre car park.

Parts of the school date to 1580 and it is a fine example of an early timber building. Among the exhibits on display in the museum is a copy of the first ever Test Match score card. This was for Australia versus England played at Melbourne during the series of 1876-77. The first entry reads

N. Thompson bowled Hill 1

Allen Hill played for Leyland Cricket Club and it was he who took the first ever test match wicket. Leyland Cricket Club was established in 1847 and was once called the nursery of Lancashire cricket.

Hill deserves his place in cricket history but this is seldom if ever acknowledged.

 ## LIVERPOOL

—— It is easy to find Liverpool's Castle Street. Stand facing the Town Hall and you are on the site of the once dominating castle but all trace of its high walls which were 9ft thick have vanished. Liverpool castle was built on the orders of the infamous King John round about 1210 but was completely demolished in 1726.

Is there any clue as to what the fortress looked like in its prime? Fortunately there is, but we must travel some distance from the city to find it and even then must ignore the oft quoted statement that it is 'nobbut a folly'.

John Hesketh Lever who made his fortune from Sunlight soap was never guilty of any act of folly in his life and he constructed Liverpool castle, its walls now lapped by the waters of Rivington reservoir and situated close to Horwich. It is appropriate that the water impounded here is piped to Liverpool.

A biography on Leverhulme makes the point that he never did things by half. He did once – he designed and had built a scaled down model of the castle just as it would have appeared at the time of its final demolition. All the details of its towers, walls, storerooms and living accommodation can still be seen. Folly it may be but it is also factual and it is possible to stand on the mini-battlements, look out over the reservoir and imagine yourself ready to repel invaders arriving at the mouth of the Mersey estuary.

This is the architectural equivalent of a mighty midget which deserves more serious consideration from historians than it has ever received.

*   *   *

As you would expect of one of Britain's major seaports, Liverpool erected a monument in 1806 to Lord Nelson. This stands at the rear of the Town Hall in the area delightfully known as Exchange Flags. It is a splendid example of the art and craft of the sculptor Richard Westmacot, the elder.

Politicians, however, do tend to react slowly although they would prefer to say that they were being 'fiscally prudent'. In any event a sugar refiner by the name of Downward quickly decided that an 'upwardly directed' monument should appear sooner rather than later and paid for a needle-like monument to be constructed. When he offered this to the city the governing body rejected it and set about erecting their own. They scoffed at Downward's gift and one councillor referred to it as a 'half Nelson'.

Downward had the 'needle' erected in his own estate garden at Springfield in Knotty Ash. The mansion has since been demolished but the garden has been retained as a public park graced by the 'half Nelson' monument bearing an inscription which reads

'Sacred to the memory of the illustrious Nelson who fell in the defence of his Country'.

LUND

—— Lund is one of the most difficult places on the Fylde to locate. It has a hall but this is in Clifton. It has a railway station but this is at Salwick and used by workers at the nearby Springfield Works of British Nuclear Fuels.

It does, however, have a church but this is modern and of little architectural merit. This accounts for the fact that it has so few visitors. But there is one interesting feature, important because there are so few artefacts relating to the Roman period, of which even students of Roman Lancashire are mostly unaware; an oblong font standing around three ft high, constructed from a Roman altar.

LYDIATE

—— Not an easy place to find, Lydiate is on a minor road about nine miles out of Liverpool on the way to Southport. Here, within strolling distance of each other, are the Scots Piper dating to the 14th century and arguably Lancashire's oldest inn and an abbey that never was.

The Scots Piper is a tiny inn but is well worth squeezing into to see the art and craft needed to construct it around the huge crook of a standing oak tree. For those prepared to enjoy more than one drink there will be time to follow the line not only of the trunk of the tree but also several of its main branches which support side walls and ceilings.

Also worth seeking out is what remains of Lydiate Old Hall and the wrongly named Lydiate Abbey which probably had no monastic associations whatever. The hall was the home of Lawrence and Catherine Ireland and the 'abbey' was actually an associated chapel dedicated to St Catherine and built around 1540. Did the Irelands obtain dressed stone from some distant abbey dissolved by Henry VIII? Burscough may well have been a possible source, but there are no facts to back up this supposition. Neither are there any to disprove it.

LYTHAM CREEK

—— Lytham is not really a seaside town but is set firmly on the estuary of the river Ribble. The settlement is mentioned in the Domesday Book under the name of Lidum and there is plenty of evidence to prove that there was a substantial Saxon settlement in the area.

This is supported by the fact that the parish church is dedicated to St Cuthbert who lived in the 6th century. The influence of this saint probably accounts for the fact that Lytham Hall (now the offices of Guardian Royal Exchange Insurance Company) and a late Georgian mansion had their origins as a farm owned by the Benedictine monks of Durham, their abbey being the final resting place of Cuthbert.

The history of the hall, the windmill on the green and its period as a seaside resort are all well documented, but Lytham Creek lies almost forgotten behind a mass of ugly warehouses.

For a long and distinguished period Lytham Creek was a prospering ship-building complex, with tug construction a speciality as were vessels called 'stern wheelers'. These were built with a shallow draught, ideally suited for use on the muddy rivers of Africa. A Lytham vessel featured in the classic black and white film *Sanders of the River*.

The last vessel to be launched at Lytham was in 1954 and was a ferry built to operate across Windermere. It is said that during the war experimental work was carried out in Lytham Creek on parts of the Mulberry harbours which played such a vital role in the D-Day landings.

LYTHAM ST ANNES

—— 'One circumstance above all must render Lytham dear to those who have a strict regard to morality – vice has not yet erected her standard here. The numerous tribes of gamblers, unhappy profligators and fashionable swindlers find employment and rapine elsewhere. Innocent recreational delights ... banish cares from the mind, whilst the salubrity of the air expels disease from the body'.

Lytham and the more modern St Annes officially joined since 1923 still have a genteel feel about them with much to interest both the historian and the naturalist. It still fits the description quoted above and written in the 1890s.

Close to St Annes pier is a monument looking rather like a war memorial and which deserves to be much better known. It celebrates the wrecking of the merchant ship *Mexico* in December 1886 on the sandbanks of the Ribble estuary between Southport and Lytham. Lifeboats were launched from both Southport and Lytham. All 13 men of the Lytham St Annes' crew were drowned and only two of the Southport crew survived. This was the worst disaster in the history of the lifeboat service, and it stimulated the development of the Royal National Lifeboat Institution (RNLI).

MANCHESTER

The river Irwell rises in the hills between Burnley and Bacup and drains most of upland Rossendale. No river has been more ill-treated by industry than the poor old Irwell which has been cut and culverted, poisoned, diverted and dammed and used as a dumping ground. What had been a major fishing river had by the mid-19th century become a stinking drain.

The Irwell divides old Salford from an upstart village called Manchester. Next time you go shopping to Manchester go in search of this old village – it is still there!

Manchester Cathedral is really an enlarged village church dating to the 15th century, but set on a Saxon foundation. It later became a collegiate church which meant that it trained priests. The kitchens obtained much of their food from the fish-rich waters of the Irwell which flows just below it although now separated by and culverted under the main road into the city. One of the exits from the churchyard was called the Dean's Gate from which the modern street of Deansgate takes its name.

Inside the church, dedicated to St Mary, St George and St Dennis is a magnificent screen and some carved seats in the choir called misericords. There is also a statue of Humphrey Chetham (1580-1653) who gave the nearby library to the people of Manchester, part of which was later established as a school for poor boys. The building itself was once the manor house of Thomas de La Warre and was given to the Collegiate Church in 1421. It became a music school only in 1969, but the library, one of the most famous in the country, is open each weekday from 9am to 5pm. Karl Marx often used this library when he lived in Manchester at the height of the Industrial Revolution. The school supplies choir boys for the cathedral and they occasionally wear the old uniform of flat hats, blue coats and yellow stockings.

Manchester has developed dramatically in the last 200 years, but for those with time to explore the cathedral area there are many reminders of the village once set in green fields and washed by the clear stream of the Irwell. Its tributaries include the Irk and the Tib which are now culverted beneath the city streets. As you walk through the city spare a thought for the streams which now flow hidden away from light and just beneath your feet.

MARTHOLME

Martholme was once a famous market in Lancashire but by the 18th century all trace had vanished. All that remains is Martholme Hall, now splendidly restored and a private residence. It can, however, be seen from a footpath and especially from a railway viaduct spanning the Calder valley.

The viaduct was constructed as part of the loop line linking Blackburn, Great Harwood, Padiham and Burnley. It opened in 1877 and was closed to passengers in 1957, and has recently been converted into a linear nature reserve. Now bluebells grow around Martholme Hall which was once overlooked by coal mines, long since closed.

The nearby Gamecock Inn was once a notorious haunt of tough colliers. The inn, however, began life as three cottages which were later converted to accommodate the drinkers but there was also stabling for 16 horses. The Gamecock was once an important coach stop between Clitheroe and Great Harwood; inside the restaurant area you can still see the stables with iron poles called boskins which were once used to separate the horse stalls.

The area around Martholme and the Gamecock looks as if it has been undisturbed for centuries but its secrets include a medieval market, Victorian coalmines and a railway, not forgetting one of Lancashire's smallest but most ancient halls.

MITTON

The importance of Mitton in the days it was a dominant village along the Ribble can be appreciated by standing on the bridge near the Aspinall Arms hotel. In dry weather the old shallow ford below can clearly be seen. This contrasts sharply with the winter scene when, after a heavy snow fall, meltwater roars through the arches of the bridge, which must have rendered the old ford useless.

Mitton village was thus often split into two before it was successfully bridged in the 18th century. Even today Great and Little Mitton are quite separate entities. At this time the Aspinall Arms was not a hotel but the boathouse of the ferrymen.

Great Mitton church and the nearby Great Mitton hall together dominate the knoll high over the river. The earliest portion of the church is the nave which is thought to have been constructed around 1270, with the chancel being added some 25 years later. The square tower had certainly been added by the early years of the 15th century and is mentioned in a document dated 1438. At the same time a side chapel, possibly a chantry, was added but this was replaced by the superb Shireburn chapel in 1594, one of the most splendid in the whole of England yet it seldom merits a mention in most guide books. Anyone wishing to trace the history of the Shireburn family which built the magnificent Stoneyhurst should visit Great Mitton church.

An alabaster tomb fashioned with delicate skill by Roily of Burton is inscribed thus:

'Here lieth the bodies of Sr. Ricrd. Sherburne Knight most Forster of ye Forrest of Bowland steward of ye Manor of Sladeburne Lieuetenants of ye Ile of Man and one of her Mats. deputie lecutes in ye Countie of Lanc. And Dame Maude his wif daught' of Sr. Ricrd Bold Knight by whom he had issue who died ye 10 of Nov. 1588 and Sr. Ricd died the 26 of Julie 1594.'

There is also a monument to his son, shown kneeling at a prayer desk facing his mother, also beautifully carved in alabaster. Understandably, with such treasures to protect, the church is kept locked but a Sunday visit or contact with the vicar or his council is easily arranged. Telephone numbers and addresses of keyholders are displayed on the church door.

The Shireburn monument in Great Mitton church.

MORECAMBE

The modern seaside resort of Morecambe has absorbed the four ancient hamlets of Heysham, Torrisholme, Bare and Poulton-le-Sands. The latter can still be found by turning inland off the promenade at the Gala bingo hall and down Lord Street to the market.

The market occupies the site of Poulton Hall which was unfortunately demolished in 1932; it would have made a splendid museum which would certainly have attracted many Americans. The original doorway has been re-erected at the rear of the town hall and carries a plaque explaining that Poulton Hall was one of the homes during the 15th and 16th centuries of the Washington family which produced George, the first and most famous president of the USA. The Washingtons also owned land at Warton near Carnforth and at Washington in County Durham.

The old doorway is almost hidden by ivy and as it is close to a graveyard is often considered to be yet another ornate tombstone. In Poulton Square there are other reminders of the old village; fishermen's cottages made of seaside cobbles, and a farmhouse bearing the initials BTL and the date 1687. A shop on the corner still sells shrimps, shellfish and fresh fish, thus maintaining a direct link with the original villagers who earned their living from the sea, rather from a steady influx of tourists.

MUCH HOOLE

In 1639, after renting a room in nearby Carr House, a young curate from Much Hoole made history in the world of astronomy.

Situated at the junction of the B5427 from Croston and the A59 Preston to Liverpool road, this brick and stone house was built in 1613 by Thomas and Andrew Stones for their brother John who was a sheep farmer. The inscription on the wall reads 'Thomas Stones of London, haberdasher, and Andrewe Stones of Amsterdam merchant, hath builded this house of their owne charges and giveth the same unto their brother John Stones, Anno Domini 1613 Lans'. The whole family fortune was based upon their wool and haberdashery business which was European in scale.

Carr House.

From his rented room Jeremiah Horrocks, one of the founders of modern astronomy, saw a black spot move across the face of the sun. This was the first time that the transit of the planet Venus had ever been plotted. There is a memorial recording that at 3.15pm on Sunday 24th November 1639 Horrocks, only 21 at the time, had made his permanent mark on the history of science. He projected the sun's image by means of a telescope onto a piece of paper and then plotted the passage of Venus across it. This proved for the first time, that during its orbit Venus actually passed between the earth and the sun. Although seemingly a simplistic explanation Horrocks' work involved inspired mathematical calculations.

He knew, as did all astronomers of the period, that Venus transits are very rare and only occur every 120 years or so. It is not even this simple, however, and it was Horrocks who discovered that the transits did not occur once but twice, the second eight years after the first. Young Jeremiah knew of a transit in 1631 which no one had been able to see in Europe because the sun was below the horizon and so he was ready in 1639 to prove the truth of his calculations. What Jeremiah Horrocks would have achieved had he not died in 1641 we can only imagine – he may well have been as famous as Newton or Galileo. Horrocks' calculations tells us that no transits will occur in the present century but can be expected in 2004 and 2012.

Although Horrocks' memory has a place of honour very close to Isaac Newton in Westminster Abbey, neither Carr House nor the nearby church at Much Hoole are on the tourist map, and neither the house nor the memorials in Much Hoole church receive the attention they deserve. There is a fine stained glass window in the church and the present vicar the Revd Harry Pugh has made strenuous efforts to have Horrocks properly remembered. He stimulated Dr Allan Chapman of Wadham College, Oxford to write a booklet on the discovery made at Carr House and this is on sale in the church.

NELSON

Nelson is a modern textile town which takes its name from the Lord Nelson hotel built because of and situated close to the railway. Prior to the arrival of the 'steam carriages' there were two attractive hamlets situated on the hillside overlooking the modern town.

Little and Great Marsden were within the manor controlled by the de Walton family who lived at Marsden Hall until they ran out of heirs in 1912.

The local authority purchased the estate, created Marsden Park but sadly demolished most of the hall. One important section was left and this now forms part of a restaurant.

Nearby is a unique sundial dating from 1841 and which now seldom gets more than a cursory glance. It is, however, a unique structure and has spike-like indicators on it which give details of the time in many parts of the world including Jerusalem, Calcutta, London, Moscow, Ceylon, Buenos Aires and perhaps significantly Fort Nelson in the USA.

The modern road connecting Nelson with Colne in one direction and Burnley in the other runs along the valley bottom; the old high road still exists but like the Marsden Sundial has kept its secret nooks and crannies for those with the time and energy to seek them out.

*   *   *

Carr Hall Lane in Nelson cuts between two housing estates and a modern bypass which carries traffic between Padiham and Nelson. The hall has been demolished but its gatehouse can still be seen among the modern houses. The drive which once led up to the hall remains and its most interesting feature is in the fields around it and concerns the position of a number of mature trees.

Many local men fought in the battle of Waterloo and soon after the victory trees were planted and arranged in battle order. Splendid oaks which still stand mark the observation points of battle stations of the victorious generals. Other trees relate to the foot soldiers. Carr Hall Lane now never receives a second glance but is well worth a visit to see this unique tree war memorial dating to 1815.

NEWCHURCH-IN-PENDLE

One of the most attractive villages on the side of Pendle Hill is Goldshaw Booth which was given a new church in the 15th century, resulting in its permanent change of name.

The church has a splendid tower and below the clock an eye has been carved. The 'eye of God' is said to have been provided so that the congregation at prayer could be sure that an eye was kept on Old Nick!

There are a number of flat gravestones in the churchyard but these have not always rested in peace. The Kirk gang, a group of cut-throats with a name and reputation as rough and tough as Jesse James in the Wild West of America rampaged around East Lancashire. The Kirk gang used to hide their loot beneath the flat stones following their regular raids on the outlying farmsteads.

It seems that the Witches of Pendle were also not averse to doing a Burke and Hare act. In the Lancashire witch trial of 1612 James Device testified that Old Mother Chattox took four teeth and three scalps from the dead at Newchurch. Alice Nutter's grave is reputedly at Newchurch but most think that this good lady, who lived at Roughlee Hall, was executed at Lancaster for her part in the witches' brew of 1612.

Before readers are frightened away from Newchurch in case darkness comes early there are more attractive features. There is a sundial in the churchyard and the interior of the church is dominated by a unique set of fluted pillars; a 17th century silver chalice is also a joy.

A famous resident of Newchurch was Jonas Moore (1617-1679) (no relation of Patrick!) who was so highly regarded as an astronomer that he was appointed as a tutor to James II. He was also one of the surveyors in charge of the draining of the Fens and a founder member of the Royal Observatory.

It seems quite appropriate that Moore, who well knew the Eye of God, should become famous for watching the stars! Close to the village is the little known remnants of a Bronze Age stone circle which may have been a tomb or perhaps an ancient astronomical calender.

 ## Noggarth Cross

—— Situated between the village of Worsthorne near Burnley and Haggate close to the Roggerham Gate Inn is the remnant of the Noggarth Cross. It is said to have been placed in this position to hold down a particularly mischievous boggart, which is the Lancastrian term for a spirit.

This is, however, one of several crosses on local moorlands which were set up to guide medieval travellers across the desolate moorland paths. They were gradually forgotten as lowland areas were drained and new roads subsequently built.

 ## Old Langho

—— One of Lancashire's forgotten villages is Old Langho which has been isolated by the construction of a series of roads between Blackburn, Preston, Whalley and Clitheroe.

It is set on the Roman road into Ribchester and was also one of the tracks used by the monks of Whalley Abbey. There is a local legend suggesting that at the time of the Reformation some monks, who were being hunted, had themselves sealed inside one of the cavity walls of what is now the Black Bull Hotel. Their friends who had carried out the sealing of the hideaway failed to return and the bones of the brethren of Whalley are said to be still there.

What is beyond dispute is that the old church with its exterior bell tower was constructed of masonry taken from

Whalley Abbey after it had been dissolved in 1536. Some of the windows have obviously been brought intact from the abbey. The church was completed in 1557 and was restored by Thomas Carr, a prosperous barrister based at the Middle Temple in London. His descendants are all buried in the churchyard and must feel at peace here in this now remote village which is held in a gentle time warp.

OVERTON

—— Visitors to Overton feel entitled to ask why the church should be situated so far from the village.

Because of the change of the shape of the coastline, with erosion in some areas and the deposition of silt in others, the village buildings had to be moved. This left the church of St Helen, constructed on a mound and overlooking the Lune estuary, in splendid isolation.

It has been suggested, although without proof, that Overton is Lancashire's oldest church but close examination shows why this theory arose. The doorway is Anglo-Norman and has been dated to between 1050 and 1140. The west wall is even older being possibly 9th century and quite likely to outlast the rest of the church as it is more than four ft thick.

The area of saltmarsh around the church is a spectacular place for birdwatching. Redshank, curlew, shelduck, knot and dunlin are all regularly seen and in spring migrating green-shanks are a feature.

No doubt the birdlife hereabouts inspired the one-time landlord of the Ship Inn in the village to gather together one of the most comprehensive collections of stuffed wild birds and eggs. These are still there perched on shelves and gazing down from the bars and the walls are lined with glass-fronted oak cases full of specimens.

This cross between a pub and a museum annoys many conservationists but Victorian naturalists gathered lots of valuable information on natural history without the benefit of high quality binoculars and cameras. Their specimens were obtained for study by shooting and there was a saying that 'what's shot is history whilst what's missed is a mystery.'

The Norman doorway of Overton church.

PARBOLD

A few years ago during a series of radio programmes on the history of Kent's windmills my host sympathised that Lancashire had no windmills apart from those in the Fylde which the 19th-century journalist Allan Clarke described graphically as 'Windmill Land'. What happened to the many windmills which must have been essential to the county's economy from the late Middle Ages to the mid-19th century?

Many have gone, and even the sites of most are all but forgotten whilst a few have survived because a secondary use has been found for them. One of my favourites is at Parbold right on the banks of the Leeds to Liverpool canal and not far from the M6. The mill is now an integral part of the Mill Lane Conservation area with its stout tower, now used as an upmarket fabric shop, but still firmly and delightfully attached to the miller's house. The present owner explained how little conversion had been needed but by the time work started most of the internal machinery and also the sails had long gone.

A walk along the towpath can be a delight for botanists because apart from the native plants there are also foreign imports such as pineapple mayweed, rosebay willow herb and evening primrose which all arrived from North America as seeds mixed in with the raw materials, especially cotton,

The windmill tower at Parbold.

carried from Liverpool docks along the cut.

Architectural canalside reminders can also be seen in the delightful old shops which once served the bargees, an old inn appropriately called the Windmill and a gaggle of old warehouses now converted into flats. No wonder Parbold is still popular with boat enthusiasts who tie up their colourful barges in a cluster around the mill. The pity is that only water borne travellers seem to appreciate the joys of this stretch of canal and the early 19th-century windmill which overlooks it.

PENDLETON

———— Pendleton, situated off the modern A59 between Whalley and Clitheroe and cut in half by a channelled brook, is both a pretty village and a working community. In the main street, between the cottages with their mullioned windows, are dairy farms, in which the rhythmic beat of milking machines mingles with the lowing of cows and the chattering of the nearby stream over its pebbled bed. Visiting motorists should be prepared to be patient if their way is blocked by cows being taken to milking.

The church and its associated school, now used as a residential centre for youth groups, dates from 1847; until then, Pendleton folk had to take one of the many green paths over the fields to the church and school in Whalley.

Pendleton receives few visitors but the nearby hamlet of Wymondhouses on the old track to Wiswell is even more remote. Here in this moorland hamlet on the foothills of Pendle Hill, Thomas Jollie (1629-1703) founded the first Congregational church in the area. No doubt he chose Wymondhouses because it was so isolated at a time when those who chose not to conform to Church of England doctrine were far from popular.

Jollie began his ministry at St James church at Altham but like many Puritans he was expelled when Charles II was restored in 1660. Eventually some semblance of toleration was established and at nearby Barrow just off the new A59 Whalley to Clitheroe road is found the Jollie Memorial chapel.

At Wymondhouses, where occasional but not well publicised outdoor services still celebrate his ministry, Jollie is commemorated only by a plaque.

Pickup Bank

This tiny hamlet, once fed by a network of packhorse tracks, is perched on a breezy hillside between Blackburn and Darwen, dotted with sheep farms and old shepherds' cottages, many now restored. At the centre of the hamlet is the imposing Old Rosin's inn, the name of which derives from the resin used around the turn of the century to polish the building's dance floor and also the musical instruments. Local people called the inn 'Old Rosin's' and this name was adopted in place of the former name, the Duke of Wellington.

Pickup Bank overlooks a fertile valley lined with trees which screen disused mills and their ponds, known locally as lodges and which provided water for the steam engines. Prior to steam little hillside streams powered small waterwheels. Pickup Bank has not always been so remote and once lay on the packhorse route connecting the weavers' cottages with the Cloth Halls as far away as Colne, Hebden Bridge and Halifax.

The man in charge of a packhorse team was known as the Jagger, and one of the ancestors of the most famous Rolling Stone once earned his living on the stony packhorse trails of old England.

Pickup Bank, even when working at full pressure, was always secluded by folds of hills, but its name is now mainly remembered because of 'Old Rosins'.

Pilling

The name Pilling actually derives from the Celtic words for a small creek and so presumably there was once a small harbour here. All traces of this have gone and the visitors who flock to the nearby Fylde coast ignore Pilling.

If you want action, noise, amusement arcades, busy pubs, candy floss and white knuckle rides then you are right to avoid Pilling. If on the other hand you want sea breezes, rich and varied wildlife, and sweeping views of meadow, marsh and sea then this is the place to be.

Apart from its natural beauty, Pilling has an often unrecognised place in history. Modern ecclesiastical historians often list Pilling church as of little interest but fail to mention a second church and one which is of worldwide interest.

The two churches are linked by a pleasant little pathway and there is ample parking adjacent to a sports field. This is close to the older of the two churches, both of which are dedicated to St John the Baptist.

The old church is kept locked these days, but a notice on the wall indicates where the key can be obtained. Although the interior is interesting and well maintained by the Redundant Churches Fund, it is the exterior which carries the main feature of interest. On the wall near the porch is a sundial dedicated to the memory of the Revd George Holden who was the vicar here between 1758 and 1767. His gift to mankind was the invention of tide tables and his mathematical genius is celebrated by the inscription.

George Holden was in an ideal place to study the tide and its devastating effect upon those who failed to appreciate its strength and timing. The Pilling area of coastline, although flatter, sandier and not so scenically dramatic as that around Devon, Cornwall or North Yorkshire was just as much a hotbed for smugglers and wreckers. These evil folk worked hard and cunningly to lure unwary ships carrying valuable cargoes onto the treacherous sands.

Nobody who has ever relied upon a set of tide tables should miss paying a visit to Pilling. Choose a day of high wind and pounding tide; you will then almost certainly be on your own. Stand by the sundial and give thanks to one of Lancashire's unsung heroes, George Holden – the man who did not tame the tide but showed us all how to live with the threat of the sea by accurately predicting its movements.

PLEASINGTON

―――― Pleasington is a very pleasant name for a very pleasant and largely rural suburb of Blackburn. Dominating the settlement is the priory – not a parish church but the Roman Catholic church of St John the Baptist.

If you ask almost anyone to list their top twenty favourite churches in Lancashire I doubt if any would include Pleasington Priory and few would even know where or what it is.

Its dominant feature is the magnificent window over the entrance and which is fine enough to be the pride of many a cathedral. The building is historic in the sense that it was built around 1820, a period when the religious laws passed against Roman Catholics in the reign of Elizabeth I were only just being relaxed.

After this period Catholics worshipped openly but obviously all their churches had become Anglican parish churches. Money was scarce and the construction of such graceful and magnificent buildings was a rare luxury.

Churches, like good wine and whisky, mature slowly and perhaps in time Pleasington Priory will be appreciated for what it is – an architectural treasure.

POULTON-LE-FYLDE

——— Poulton only had le-Fylde added to its name when the post office started handling large numbers of business letters and confusion arose because of another Lancashire Poulton; Poulton-le-Sands which is now part of modern Morecambe.

These days Poulton-le-Fylde is a small but delightful market town often ignored by tourists because of the close proximity of brash and breezy Blackpool. One side of the pedestrianised square is overlooked by the church of St Chad, always a delight but seen at its sprightly best in the spring when it is surrounded by a carpet of crocuses.

At the other end of the square is a large 17th-century cross, a set of fish stones, stocks and a whipping post. During the 17th and 18th centuries Poulton was a vital port co-ordinating the activities of Wardleys and Skippool Creeks, both now almost forgotten backwaters. When Poulton was a hard-working seaport it needed its stocks and its whipping post to deal with the law breakers, its stones to display the fish for sale and also its market cross from which declarations could be delivered by the town crier.

This impressive collection of the town's history forms a unique combination which seldom receives the attention it deserves.

PRESTON

——— Situated in the Avenham Park area of Preston is the unusual Old Tram Bridge, a rather controversial name because though most locals accept that it is indeed an old tram bridge a few stubborn folk insist that it was designed by Benjamin Outram – hence Outram Bridge!

The bridge carried a horse-drawn railway which linked the Lancaster Canal terminus in Preston to the summit of the Leeds to Liverpool Canal between Bamber Bridge and Brindle. The original intention was to build an aqueduct and carry a canal from the Lancaster Canal to the Leeds to Liverpool. This, however, proved too expensive as the Ribble valley was not easy to drain.

There was indeed a Tram Road which passed under Preston's Fishergate via a tunnel and then over the Ribble near Avenham Park. It is still possible to trace the line of the embankment used by the tram road. I put this to a local who objects to the old tram theory

'Twern't a tram – it 'ad 'osses on it – an' oo sez old Outram niver bilt it.'

Whoever is right, this is a little known part of Lancashire's history, and either or both explanations will do.

*   *   *

Preston has long been an important town as it stood at a crossing point of the river Ribble. This was at the spot now occupied by Penwortham Bridge.

Modern Preston has some fine buildings including the splendid Harris Museum and Art Gallery, but I am always sad when I think about the once proud docks. In the 1950s I travelled aboard a vessel bringing timber into Preston Docks as she sailed slowly up the straight canalised river Ribble, carried along on a high tide. She berthed beneath a forest of towering cranes. The smell of diesel and sea water was diluted by the resinous smell of timber which was one of the main imports in latter years. After disembarking into the busy heart of dockland I was taken to a first division football match at Deepdale and watched Matthews of Blackpool match his skills with those of Finney of Preston. At the end of a perfect day I thought that nothing would ever change.

As I write Blackpool and Preston football teams are hidden in the depths of the lower divisions and the docks have closed to serious trade as Britain looks towards Europe rather than to America, thus putting the west coast ports at a disadvantage.

Although Preston had landing areas in the 14th century and these were more important than Liverpool during the 16th, the main efforts to deepen the navigation channel did not begin until the 19th century when cotton was king in Preston. While the new docks were being constructed Neolithic axe heads and arrows were discovered as well as an ancient canoe. Also discovered were the bones of long extinct animals including the antlers of huge deer.

The main docklands complex was completed about 1890 and an integral part of the system was the ship-breaking yard of Thomas Ward. There was another of Ward's 'ship cemeteries' at Morecambe where the Dome complex now stands. One of the most famous vessels smashed to bits at Preston was the White Star Liner the *Adriatic*. Launched in 1872 she was once the pride of the fleet and broke the Atlantic crossing time in 1873 whilst carrying 900 passengers and crew in great comfort. In 1899 she was broken up and many of her luxury fittings were used to decorate the Adriatic Dance Hall in Preston, itself now confined to history.

Throughout the early 1980s Preston docks were a sad sight but in recent years the area has been given an impressive face lift. Many visitors, however, seem reluctant to accept the progress being made. I wandered about the Riverside Business Centre, had a quiet lunch in the Waterfront Hotel and looked out across the dock towards old buildings now converted into posh residential flats. The name posh takes us back to the days of luxury liners when the rich had port cabins outward (p.o.) and starboard cabins on the way home (s.h.). This meant that the luxury cabins had the best of the sun, neither too hot nor too cold. Port Out Starboard Home gives us POSH.

Looking towards the town the docklands are overlooked by the soaring white steeple of St Warburg's church and alongside the marina is a large car park. A road separates this car park from a supermarket. In the summer the Docklands and river Ribble can be explored aboard small motor vessels and Preston Marina is coming through its depression but its attractions are still overshadowed by its derelict reputation of the 1980s.

*   *   *

Most people have heard of Richard Arkwright but few know where his house is, and hardly anybody remembers poor old

Dicky Turner who first used the term 'teetotal'.

Arkwright was born in Preston in 1732 and spent some time in Bolton as a barber. He was a born inventor who by all accounts was famous for the manufacture of wigs; it was, however, as an innovator in textile machinery that he achieved fame. He set up a workshop in a house near Preston's parish church of St Peter's, where in 1769 he built his now famous water frame. The local artisans made life so uncomfortable for the man whose machine could do the work of eight without getting tired that he moved to Nottingham. There Richard Arkwright achieved fame and made his fortune. His talents should be commemorated by the setting up of a museum in Preston and Arkwright's House, now being restored as a conference centre, would be ideal as a museum. I for one would celebrate with a glass of bubbly if this came to pass.

This would make Dicky Turner stir in his grave, situated in St Peter's churchyard. Dicky's memorial is inscribed on his headstone which reads that he was the 'author of the word TEETOTAL, as applied to abstinence from all intoxicating liquors, who departed this life on the 27th day of October 1846, aged 56 years'. Apparently Dicky was a reformed alcoholic with a pronounced stutter who addressed a crowd of drunks as being in need of

'st-st-sto-ping supping and going t-t-t-tee-to-to-total'.

RADCLIFFE

—— Radcliffe near Bury was a product of the Industrial Revolution, but in Anglo-Saxon times the hill of red sandstone above the Irwell and close to its junction with its tributary the Roch was settled. Its old name was Rate-Clive, meaning the red cliff. The Normans tried to rename it Rougemont, but the Saxons hereabouts were stubborn – they still are – and the old name remains.

The Radcliffe family dominated the Bury area for almost 500 years and 'William Radcliffe of the Tower' was called to the Grand Inquest of the County of Lancaster in the year 1211. Although the precise nature of his crime was not designated, it appears that he had been 'implicated in treason'.

The remains of the Radcliffe tower now lie in ruins and almost forgotten whilst the old deer park is smothered beneath a concrete jungle. It was politics which made the family, and politics which destroyed them. One Radcliffe took the side of John the evil regent against Richard the Lionheart, for which indiscretion he was luckily only fined. By 1403 they were back on the right side, because Henry IV gave James de Radcliffe permission 'to embattle and fortify' his house on the Irwell. By the time of Richard III, however, the family were back once more on the wrong side of the political blanket and in his play Shakespeare records the event for posterity. We should remember, however, that the playwright lived in Tudor England and therefore could not afford to give Richard III, the last Plantagenet, credit for anything.

> The Catte, the Ratte and Lovel our dog
> Ruleth all England under a Hogge

In this Shakespeare refers to Catesby as a cat (Guy Fawkes, living in the next century, was a Catesby and related to the Radcliffes at Ordsall Hall in Salford) and the Ratte was of course Radcliffe himself; Lord Lovel had a dog on his family crest and poor old Richard III of the Plantagenet line was shown as a pig, which must have delighted Elizabeth Tudor. They eventually recovered from Bosworth and as a result of a series of sensible marriages a Radcliffe became Earl of Sussex in the reign of Henry VIII and another the Earl of Derwentwater when he married an illegitimate daughter of Charles II in 1688. The family became extinct because they again meddled in politics and supported the Stuart rebellions of 1715 and 1745. Several young Radcliffes literally lost their heads during these turbulent times.

The Radcliffes have left one true reminder in the form of an alabaster tombstone in the church showing a knight and his lady. They have also left one legend concerning a jealous stepmother ridding herself of her husband's only daughter by having her killed and baked in a pie. She was helped by the head cook but a faithful page-boy tried to save the lass:

> Oh save her life good master cook
> And make your pies of me
> For pity's sake do not destroy
> My lady with your knife
> You know she is her father's joy
> For Christ's sake save her life.

Ellen of Radcliffe was still butchered but the truth came out and her enemies did not escape.

Then all in black this lord did mourne
And for his daughter's sake
He judged her cruell stepmother
To be burnt at the stake
Likewise he judged the master cook
In boiling lead to stand:
And made the simple scullion boy
The heir to all his land.

RAINHILL

—— Some three miles from Prescot, crossed by numerous and noisy railway tracks and the old A57 road linking Warrington and Liverpool, is Rainhill which is rightly said to be the birthplace of the steam locomotive.

Rainhill station, once known as Kendricks Cross, was the scene of the famous Locomotive Trials of the 6th October 1829, won by Stephenson's *Rocket*. Other locomotives tried to puff and clank their way to glory and an impressive competitor was John Ericsson's *Novelty*, one of the cylinders of which can be seen in the waiting room at Rainhill station.

Close by is Stephenson's Skew Bridge said to be the first road bridge to cross a railway. Actually the bridge was designed by the railway engineer George Findlay, but perhaps the attraction and close presence of Stephenson was too much to resist. You would have thought that George had enough memorials whilst poor old Findlay still has none!

Although now swamped by the present Merseyside conurbation the original trials track is marked by plaques at Rainhill and at the site of the now demolished Lea Green station. *Rocket* reached the then phenomenal speed of 24 miles per hour without its boiler exploding but unfortunately it also knocked down and killed William Huskinson, the MP for Liverpool. Thus the *Rocket* had a day of both triumph and tragedy.

RAWCLIFFE HALL

—— Now based around a country club and caravan site Rawcliffe Hall is inaccessible to all but the patrons of this lovely spot. Those with a genuine interest in Lancashire's history, however, are always made most welcome and there are several explorers of the county who now enjoy restful summer weekends at Rawcliffe Country Club purely because of an initial interest in the hall.

There was a dwelling here from Saxon times onwards but written records began in 1154 when the Butlers were listed as the Hereditary Cup Bearers to Henry II. Inside the hall are stained glass windows which depict this monarch's coat of arms and also shown is the tower of the church at nearby St Michael's-on-Wyre. During 1956, restoration of the church revealed some impressive painted wall murals and these have been further protected during the mid-1990s.

The Butlers of Rawcliffe Hall were always ardent Catholics and they lost their inheritance during the fraught days of the Spanish Armada. Prior to this 'grand enterprise' two Butlers gave protection to Cardinal Allen.

Allen was born in 1532 at Rossall (now a famous public school) and after being educated at Oxford's Oriel College became a Catholic priest. After Mary's reign it became impossible for him to remain in England; he lectured in the Low Countries, then went to Rome where he became a thorn in Elizabeth's side. She cannot really be blamed for seeking vengeance as he described his lawful queen as 'an incestuous bastard, an infamous, depraved, accursed, excommunicated heretic, the very shame of her sex, the chief spectacle of sin and abomination in this our age and the only poison, calamity and destruction of our noble Church, a filthy wicked and illiberal creature'.

When Allen temporarily returned to England in 1562 Elizabeth hunted him around the Rossall area and in the nearby halls of Mains and Rawcliffe. His friends were faithful and suffered badly by supporting him, but the Cardinal was never caught and he died in his own bed at the age of 63.

The Butlers never recovered from the days of the Armada when even the locals they had known through many generations did not like the support given to the Papal army. The family may have gone but thankfully their hall remains surrounded by happy holiday-makers at peace in their caravans, many of them unaware of the Saxon, Norman, Plantaganet and Tudor history at their fingertips.

 **READ**

The modern A671 between Padiham and Whalley passes alongside the extensive parkland of Read Hall. The present Georgian mansion replaced a medieval hall which was the home of the Nowells.

Roger Nowell played his part in the local politics of 1612 as he was the magistrate who sent the Pendle Witches and especially Alice Nutter to trial (see *Newchurch-in-Pendle*).

Alexander Nowell (1597-1602), however, was right at the centre stage of the fiery ecclesiastic politics of Tudor England. He became Dean of St Paul's and in 1588 preached the sermon to Elizabeth at the service to celebrate the defeat of the Spanish Armada. It did not go down very well by all accounts but the crafty cleric had a way of avoiding trouble and thus kept his head (literally) through the reigns of Henry VIII, Bloody Mary, the child Edward VI and Elizabeth. He died in his bed at the age of over ninety. His usual escape route was to disappear on fishing trips. Whilst angling he is said to have 'invented' bottled beer but it should really be regarded as a happy accident. He always took ale and food when fishing and kept his drink cool in the river. He was once called away urgently and forgot his ale. When he returned a few days later the added 'fizz' gave the ale a new sparkle and bottled beer was born.

Because of these two interesting characters the one event of national importance which took place at Read itself has largely been forgotten. The battle of Read Bridge is sometimes described as a minor skirmish. It was far more than that!

On Thursday 20th April 1643 a band of Royalists, possibly as many as 2,000 well organised troops under the command of the Earl of Derby were ambushed at Read Bridge by a much smaller force of Parliamentarians led by Captain Ashton. The Royalists were never a force in Lancashire after this event and it was the turning point of the Civil War in the county. The Earl of Derby was well regarded by the Cavaliers and his humiliation here may well have had a significant knock-on effect in other regions.

Read Bridge is not easy to find as it is on the old road to Whalley via Portfield on the site of a Roman marching camp. The bridge is situated above the village on a minor road. There is a small parking area close to the bridge and a footpath leads down to Sabden Brook, a scene which has changed little, if at all, since the fateful ambush.

RIBCHESTER

—— Situated opposite the De Tabley Arms near Ribchester Bridge, and missed by all motorists and most walkers, is New Hall. Despite its name the hall is actually old, and was built in 1665 as a dower house by the Talbot family. The name was given to distinguish it from their main house which was the nearby Samlesbury Old Hall.

In 1905 the house was described as semi-derelict and although it was still lived in its roof was almost gone and the house was smothered, perhaps even held together, by ivy. It had almost crumbled away by the mid-1980s but was then purchased by a local builder. New Hall is now 'new' once more and has been splendidly restored stone by original stone. It even has a block over the entrance bearing the original carving of a 'Talbot dog', a now extinct hunting dog, which was an integral part of the family coat of arms.

Here risen, like a phoenix from the ashes, is one of Lancashire's finest examples of a mid-17th century house and though now very much a private dwelling, once you know where it is it can easily be seen from the road without intrusion.

RIMINGTON

—— Pendle Hill is famous throughout Britain for its witches but only one of its villages is known throughout the Christian world. Rimington is renowned not for a person or an event but for a hymn tune.

Francis Duckworth was born on Christmas Day 1862 and by the time he died in 1941 the hymn tune which he named after his home village was already one of the world's best known. Most of those who know and love the tune do not know the village after which it was named.

When he was five Francis moved with his family to Stopper Lane where they ran the village shop. This was next door to the Wesleyan chapel which is now a private house.

The family were all devout Christians, especially Uncle Joe

whose favourite phrase was 'Jesus shall reign where'er the sun'. This made a lasting impression on young Francis who in 1904 wrote

'Jesus shall reign where'er the sun
Doth his successive journeys run,
His Kingdom stretch from shore to shore,
Till moons shall wax and wane no more.'

Francis Duckworth did not have an easy life as his mother died when he was only 12 and he then worked for his brother as a printer. In 1889 he opened a grocer's shop in Colne. He was a fine musician and one of the best organ players in the district. When his hymn was published in 1904 he called the tune Rimington and it first took Lancashire and Yorkshire by storm before spreading to the rest of Britain and the world.

It was first heard during the Colne Whitsuntide processions, 22 massed choirs then sang it at Pendleton on the side of Pendle Hill, 20,000 people joined voice at Nelson whilst at Halifax over in Yorkshire the congregation was doubled. Many recordings were made during Francis Duckworth's lifetime, and Rimington soon became a particular favourite of the brass bands for which this area has long been famous.

A plaque in the village records the man and his tune and a few bars are inscribed on the tomb of Francis Duckworth, tucked away and all but forgotten in the churchyard of St Mary the Virgin at nearby Gisburn.

RIVINGTON PIKE

—— Many people think that Rivington Pike is only the name of a hill – it is not. The Pike is marked precisely by a tower, but which tower is the true Pike because there are actually two buildings on the skyline? Most visitors opt for the wrong one simply because it is the easiest to see from the road. The best approach is along the narrow twisting route signed off the main Blackburn to Bolton road near Belmont.

Close to the summit of the hill stands a tall, slim tower which is often wrongly identified as the Pike, but this is in fact a lower and more squat structure situated higher up the hill though much more difficult to see. It was built by John Andrews in 1733 to prove his ownership of Rivington Manor which he bought in 1729.

There had been a cairn of stones on the hill from at least the 12th century when a chain of beacons stretched across the country to warn of invasion. Their use continued right up to the development of reliable radio, but some beacons are still lit to celebrate national events, the last occasion being the wedding of Prince Charles in 1981. Other northern lights in the chain included Ashurst's Beacon, Billinge Hill and Winter Hill. It is known from documents of the time that the Rivington Beacon was torched by mistake on July 9th 1588 at a time when England's Protestants were being threatened by Philip of Spain's Catholic Armada.

The tower on the Pike itself was used for a while as a shooting lodge and although Lancashire's moors have never been so famous as those across the border in Yorkshire there were good grouse bags recorded in Victorian times. The well marked footpath up to the peak still pushes through tufts of heather from which the red grouse calls its familiar 'go back – go back' sound, and over which kestrels frequently hover and hen harriers are occasionally seen.

But what about the second tower – what is it if not the pike marker? It is in fact a pigeon tower which was part of the residence built on and around Rivington Hill by Lord Lever-hulme.

Born in 1851 into a nonconformist family in Bolton, William Hesketh Lever joined his father's grocery business at the age of 15 but by 1872 he was running the enterprise. His particular talent was marketing and he soon moved into producing his own products obviously at competitive prices. His main success lay in the production of Sunlight soap, which he adver-tised aggressively.

He amassed such a considerable fortune that he was able to build Port Sunlight, on the banks of the Mersey, for his workforce and to purchase and develop the Rivington estate for himself.

His home on the hillside was called Roynton Cottage but it was an impressive structure surrounded by magnificent gardens and overlooked by the pigeon tower. On 7th July 1913 when Mr and Mrs Lever (Lord and Lady Leverhulme by this time) were dining with King George V and his queen at the home of Lord Derby, a suffragette named Edith Rigby set fire to Roynton Cottage. A considerable part of the building was of timber and it was soon reduced to ashes.

Only the pigeon tower remains intact today but below it are the foundations of the cottage and footpaths wind about cascades of water, shrubs and flowers which still bear witness to the expertise of Lord Leverhulme's gardeners.

Both the Pike and the pigeon towers are obviously a part of Lancashire's history and the climb to reach either of them is always well worth the effort.

🌿 ROCHDALE

——— In 1844 a village shop in Toad Lane, Rochdale made history. Now a small museum, this building was the first co-operative store, formed under the socialist reformer Robert Owen (1771-1858), with principles formulated by a local group, the Rochdale Pioneers. They would not allow any form of credit which was at that time the undoing of many other like minded groups intent upon serving working-class families. What these pioneers did was quite the reverse. Each shopper was allowed membership of the store and paid in hard cash but the profits were to be divided – the more you spent the more profits you would receive.

This was the beginning of the 'divi' scheme which then spread throughout Britain and the world. The co-op was thus able to purchase in bulk and force market prices down. This technique led to the formation of modern supermarkets.

The co-op was first called the Rochdale Equitable Pioneers and they eventually evolved their own bank and played a leading role in the education system from Victorian times onwards.

The Toad Lane Museum is seen by very few yet still known, if only by name, to the rest of the world.

Nearby is a structure which is unique to Britain. A postbox has been incorporated into a roadside lamp standard and is beautifully restored and painted.

🌿 ROUGHLEE HALL

——— No event in Lancashire's history has generated more interest than the witch trials of 1612. Visitors pour into Pendle to look for Malkin Tower at Blacko which does not now exist

– then they go on to Newchurch-in-Pendle in search of Alice Nutter's grave which although marked with her name may or may not be her last resting place.

Travelling from Blacko to Newchurch visitors pass Roughlee Hall, which was Alice Nutter's home but is now converted into private residences and hidden behind a modern yet selective housing estate.

The Tudor house is in an excellent state of repair with mullioned windows, and not spoiled by its conversion. Witches are normally regarded as having been toothless old hags living in hovels so it comes as something of a surprise to find a gentlewoman so accused. Could it be possible that Alice Nutter was framed? Researches suggest that this might well have been the case. There were two rival old hags in Pendle – Mothers Chattox and Demdike, each of whom had a group of unsavoury supporters. Both camps implicated Alice Nutter in a web of superstition. She was brought before Roger Nowell of Read, a magistrate who was a Protestant and a landowner. In 1612 he was embroiled in a lawsuit over land rights with Alice Nutter who was an ardent Catholic. To hear the mass in 1612 was punishable by death. Nowell accused her on the evidence of the two old women of attending a coven on Good Friday. Alice may have preferred to allow her trial to go ahead and remain silent because on that day she had been at mass. She preferred to die as a witch rather than betray a priest in hiding and those faithful Catholics who were with her. It is also interesting to note that following Alice Nutter's execution her legal action against Roger Nowell lapsed, leaving the magistrate in control of the disputed lands.

Roughlee Hall may therefore be misnamed – this is perhaps no witch's house but the house of a Catholic martyr and a much wronged woman. Whatever the truth, this architectural delight of a house should be more firmly set upon the trail of those tourists fascinated by the Pendle Witches, so well documented in the novels of Robert Neill and Harrison Ainsworth.

 ## RUFFORD

The National Trust administer the Old Hall at Rufford, set on the A59 road between Preston and Liverpool. It is a remarkable building in its own right, but the fact that it has a firm Shakespearian connection gives it a unique flavour to Lancashire. It is therefore something of a surprise to find that the house is known to so few within the county.

Now set idyllically on the banks of the Leeds to Liverpool Canal, which was actually dovetailed around it, Rufford dates back to the 14th century and the magnificent Great Hall with its hammer beam roof is 43 ft long and 23 ft wide. During 1996 the roof was being repaired and the curator told me that it was the stone which had to be replaced; the original timbering in a fine state of repair and as good as the day it was built.

What about this Lancastrian lad called William Shakespeare?

Lord Strange, who became the fifth Earl of Derby in 1593, was a well rounded man who enjoyed his food, the hunt, and was an exponent not only of the martial arts but of the liberal arts as well. He established a group of players and employed a writer-actor named William Shakeshafte. It is a fact that the young bard was often known by this variation and his grandfather had used this spelling. Could it just be that the first breeze of what became a Tempest had fluttered the banners of Rufford Old Hall?

SALFORD

—— 'Salford is a dirty town just outside Manchester,' I heard a man tell his companion on the Manchester train. 'There is nothing there but warehouses and run-down docks'.

Salford is actually an ancient settlement separated from Manchester by the river Irwell and which until the Industrial Revolution was by far the larger of the two, Manchester then being little more than a village. The dockland area is now called Salford Quays which have been recently restored. From what amounted to a no-go area it has become one of the north of England's success stories.

There has, however, always been more to Salford than run-down docks have suggested, and tucked away behind the web of industrial buildings is one of the most interesting old halls in the whole of England. Ordsall Hall is now a museum but it has never been given the publicity which it deserves.

There is a document referring to Ordsall in 1177 and in 1251 the estate and hall belonged to David de Hulton. At that time and until the mid-19th century Ordsall was a large country manor. In 1354 the last de Hulton died and Sir John Radcliffe inherited. It was this ambitious gentleman who began the construction of the present building.

The hall has many fascinating features including the Star Chamber wing which is a totally unspoiled 14th century masterpiece. Another period piece is the Meeting Hall of 1520 built by Sir Alexander Radcliffe. This was a successful effort to enhance his image as the High Sheriff of Lancashire.

Ordsall is said by some historians to have played its part in one of the most notorious events in British history. Robert Catesby is alleged to have travelled to Ordsall in 1605 to pursuade Sir John Radcliffe to support the Gunpowder Plot. It is thought that Guy Fawkes also visited Ordsall and to have used a secret passage leading down to the river Irwell without being seen.

The Radcliffes seem to have ridden out the after-shocks of the Gunpowder Plot and enough funds had been found to construct a brick extension to Ordsall in 1639. By the time Charles I challenged Parliament the family were once more hard up and compounded their problems by again backing the wrong side. Sir Alexander made all the wrong decisions and by the time his son John inherited the estate it was insolvent. In 1662, despite the restoration of Charles II, he was obliged to sell.

Then followed periods of ownership by the Birches, Oldfields, Stocks, Hills and Egertons before Ordsall Hall was purchased by Salford Corporation in 1959. Sensitive, extensive and expensive restorations have gradually produced a major museum which receives far too few visitors because tourists still do not accept that Salford could possibly have such an historic building.

SAMLESBURY

The origin of the word Samlesbury seems to cause historians heated debate. According to Ekwall's book of place-names it derives from the Old English sceamol which means a bench. Samlesbury Lower Hall did indeed stand on a slight ledge above the river Ribble.

Other researchers have suggested that it has Roman origins and that they called it Minerva Belisima, and later the Angles' word for a fortified place, bury, was added. Thus we have the name Belisamabury, which has in later years been reduced to Samlesbury.

Most people visit the half-timbered and beautifully restored Samlesbury Hall without ever realising that this is really the New Hall. The Old Hall, or what is left of it, is down by the river Ribble lying in a beautiful setting; it is a very important though almost forgotten part of Lancashire's history.

It is reached by following signs for Balderstone off the A59 almost opposite the gates of the British Aerospace factory and runways. This lies on land once belonging to the Southworths of Samlesbury. The signs should then be followed to Bezza nursery which is a cross between a garden centre and a history lesson.

From the elevated site of the nursery the ruined façade of Old Samlesbury Hall can be seen snuggled down by the river. It was badly damaged by invading Scots around 1320 and the Southworths decided to build a new hall away from the important river crossing. This was then set in the quiet peace of an ancient woodland, a peace only shattered by the construction of the Blackburn to Preston turnpike road in the early 1800s following which the New Hall became a coaching inn.

Bezza House also has a long and fascinating history, parts of the present building dating to the 17th century although there has probably been activity here since Saxon times.

In front of the house is a stone column which is almost certainly the shaft of an early Christian cross. This suggests that the cross marked the vital track leading to the fording point of the Ribble. Old Samlesbury Hall was probably built to protect this ford but the old Bezza cross certainly pre-dates even the Southworths' first dwelling.

*   *   *

St Leonard-the-Less – a church with such an intriguing name should not be missed and yet few visitors find it. No doubt this is because of the heavy traffic which flows along the dual carriageway from Blackburn just beyond the M6 motorway. The church is signed to the left.

For the origins of the church of St Leonard-the-Less we must go back to Norman times when a landowner called Gospatrick built a chapel-of-ease in 1185. The main church was at Walton-le-Dale and 'the lesser church' operated around Samlesbury.

From 1238 to 1537 the church was in the care of Whalley Abbey but after the dissolution St Leonard-the-Less almost became 'St Leonard-the-gone-altogether' and it was only saved when restored by the third Earl of Derby in 1558.

Inside there is an interesting structure known as an 'invasion beam' which was used to secure the door. This beam may well have saved the villagers who were hiding in the tower at the time of the Scots invasion of 1322, led by Robert the Bruce who caused havoc in northern England.

In the churchyard is a flat gravestone with the structure 'nailed down' by bars of iron. Legend suggests that in the 18th century Tom Alker's wife threatened to haunt him if he ever took another wife should she die before him. Tom did fancy somebody else and decided to fasten down his wife's spirit, just in case she raised the devil.

The grave is said to be that of a witch, but Tom Alker's fear of his first wife is much more likely. Whatever it is, the gravestone, with its inscription now faded and overgrown is part of Lancashire's history. The church of St Leonard-the-Less was underrated from the day of its consecration by its very name and its glory has probably never been given the credit which its beauty deserves.

On the river just above Samlesbury church was the old ferry which operated at least from 1379 and continued in use until 1826. The boathouse is dated to 1740 and marks have been cut into the stone window sill. RH 1771 and RH 1775 tells us the levels reached by Ribble floodwaters, and inscribed by the ferryman.

 SAWLEY

'Is there no nook of English ground secure
From rash assault?...
Plead for thy peace thou beautiful romance
Of nature; and, if human hearts be dead,
Speak passing winds; ye torrents with your strong
And constant voice, protest against the wrong'.

This verse was William Wordsworth's protest at the coming of the railway. Now we protest when they are closed and rejoice when they are re-opened.

The welcome given to the re-opening of the line between Blackburn and Clitheroe reminded me to re-read *Rambles by the Ribble*, written by William Dobson in the 1860s in which he describes his journeys by rail and how he reached his starting point by reference to the famous Bradshaw's book of time-tables.

In one ramble he describes the derelict and now almost vanished Chatburn station from which he walked along the Ribble to Sawley (or Salley abbey). He mentioned the ruin and that the abbey stone had for many years been used as an unofficial quarry for the village and the surrounding district. Many local cottages and farms have inscribed stones incorpo-rated into their structure whilst larger bits of masonry were removed to construct more important buildings. Substantial bits of Salley can now be found incorporated into the nearby Gisburn Mill and also Little Mearley Hall.

Sawley Abbey was founded by the Cistercians in 1147, was dissolved on the orders of Henry VIII in 1536 and its abbot hanged the following year for resisting the destruction of his abbey. Abbot De Trafford was hanged at Lancaster and it is said that Paslew of Whalley met the same fate outside his own abbey.

There is a delightful walk upstream from Sawley which passes below Gisburn where the Ribble is bridged near an old mill and a splendid view from the bridge near to which is the old corn mill with the miller's dwelling now a private house. Without being a nuisance to the present occupants it is easy to find the carved stones on the side wall, which were obviously once part of the abbey. One depicts the coats of arms of the Percy family who founded the abbey.

A much more substantial chunk of Sawley abbey – a lovely mullioned window – is incorporated into Little Mearley Hall. This is now a farmhouse but in such a fine state of repair that its former glory can easily be appreciated.

The track passing Little Mearley is the old monastic road from Sawley and Clitheroe to Whalley but, though beautiful, these days it is hardly used at all.

Sefton is a hamlet on the outskirts of Liverpool and is clustered around the 16th-century church dedicated to St Helen. This has a tower topped by a lofty spire which is more than 600 years old. Sefton surprisingly retains all its medieval tranquillity. Because it is so close to a major city many people seem reluctant to accept that the centre of Sefton is still an unspoiled village. At one time St Helen's was known as the cathedral of south Lancashire, and as such it deserves much more attention than it receives.

The church ceiling has been restored by 20th century craftsmen; the new bosses and moulded beams match the quality of the 16th-century screens and the ornately carved pulpit of 1635 is also magnificent. Medieval stained glass recently unearthed in the vestry has been incorporated into some of the windows, and there is a beautifully preserved display of 16th-century brasses.

The box pews are among the finest in the county. They include those once occupied by the dog whippers whose job was to exclude unwanted animals from the church and to control those brought by members of the congregation. The animals protected worshippers on their often long walks to and from church.

The church contains a couple of stone effigies of men-at-arms and a so-called 'Treacle Bible' with some mistranslations which were corrected in the Authorised Version of 1611. For example, Jeremiah 8 v 22 reads : 'There is no more triacle [the authorised version gives balm] in Gilead.' Another curious rendering occurs in Psalm 91 v 5: 'Thou shalt not need be afraid for any bugges [AV terror] by night'. The translation was the work of Miles Coverdale born in the Yorkshire Dales, who became Bishop of Exeter in 1535.

Long gone, but not quite forgotten, is the Sefton Corporation which was active in the early 19th century but never intended to be an administrative body. They are commemorated by a brass plate on a box pew bearing the inscription 'Corporation of Sephton'.

The corporation apparently worshipped at St Helen's and then retired to the nearby Punch Bowl Inn to celebrate any victory during the Peninsular War then being fought by Wellington against Napoleon's forces. The Corporation gave themselves humorous names such as Butter Weigher, Commissioner of Hackney Coaches and Window Peeper but like the modern Lions' clubs their aim was always to raise money. They used this to send comforts and especially flannel shirts to Wellington's troops. In 1940 their regalia was sent to Liverpool City Museum but unfortunately failed to survive the German bombing of the port. All that therefore remains to celebrate the corporation is the brass plaque.

SHARD BRIDGE

There was an outcry in 1993 when the Shard Toll Bridge across the river Wyre was replaced by a modern flyover. The complaints came not because of the new bridge but because the old relic of the turnpike age was demolished. Many felt that it should have been left alongside the new bridge as a monument.

Most traces of the old Shard Bridge however, have now gone and local newspapers at the time had bulging post-bags complaining that no effort was made to preserve any mementoes of the construction. The Shard Bridge Inn, however, purchased many of the artefacts including the toll board, the controlling traffic lights and many signs relating to the bridge. These are on display inside and outside the hotel and this enterprise deserves more publicity than has been the case. This is an example of Lancashire's transport history not being lost for ever, but merely disregarded. The hotel, once at the hub of the flow of traffic across the toll bridge, is now literally out on a limb and it is vital that the last remaining toll bridge upstream at Cartford should be retained.

In the car park of the inn the supports of the old bridge still remain and it is a marvellous place to watch the river with its rich bird life apparent at all states of the tide.

SILVERDALE

On the outskirts of this charming village is a tower with two names, a confusing history and strong literary connections. Gibraltar Tower, also called Lindeth Tower has been described in more than one guide book as yet another

14th-century pele tower built as a protection against the invading Scots.

Despite the intentional yet superficial resemblance, the tower was constructed by a Preston banker named Fleetwood in 1825 as a holiday home.

Lindeth has somehow failed to become a literary shrine in recent years, despite a revival of interest in the works of the early Victorian novelist Elizabeth Gaskell. Born in Knutsford, Elizabeth married a minister who worked in the run-down slums of Manchester. She was very much ahead of her time regarding her views on the place of women in society. She brought up her daughters in true Victorian tradition but also found time to write articles and novels, many of which were serialised in magazines edited by Charles Dickens, who had a very good opinion of Elizabeth Gaskell.

Lindeth was a favourite holiday haunt of Mrs Gaskell who wrote part of her novel *Cranford* in an upper room of the tower with a view over the sands of Morecambe Bay.

Silverdale has an even more illustrious literary connection because when illness struck the school for clergymen's daughters at Cowan Bridge, Charlotte and Emily Brontë were removed to Silverdale and stayed at Cove House.

Coincidentally it was Mrs Gaskell who wrote the first biography of Charlotte Brontë. If the hauntingly beautiful Silverdale, with its strong literary connections had been situated in the Cotswolds or on the coast of Devon, it would be bulging with craft shops, museums, restaurants with twee names, well signed literary walks and bouncing with visitors.

Far preferable is the sound of birds and the peace of the place, so perhaps it is as well that Silverdale's secrets are still safe.

SINGLETON

—— A man photographing the electricity sub-station in the charming little village of Singleton told me that this tiny building was Tudor. Actually it is Victorian mock-Tudor, now kept in fine repair because of the importance of the machinery inside which provides the link between the national grid and the houses of the village. A gentle hum indicates that it is reducing the huge incoming voltage ready for domestic use.

The old fire-station.

This has not always been its function because it was originally a purpose built fire-station and is the oldest such building remaining in Lancashire. Constructed in 1882 by the local landowner T. H. Miller the station was for a brigade consisting of 14 men under the control of a captain. The whole crew were volunteers drawn from the work force of Miller's estate.

In the context of our modern emergency services the horse-drawn, manually operated appliance would seem to have been almost comically cumbersome. At the time of its establishment, however, the Singleton Brigade must have been regarded as a wondrous saviour of life and T. H. Miller was considered, quite rightly, as a most enlightened man.

The half-timbered black and white building still has the elaborate inscriptions on its walls and its doors are still painted in striking scarlet.

Looking at it I appreciate that this is a little known piece of our hidden history, but allow myself a smile at the thought of the old-time music hall Lancastrian comedian Rob Wilton. He had a sketch based in a fire-station in which he asked a terrified runner reporting a fire if he could go back and keep the blaze going until he had rounded up the crew and harnessed the horse!

SLAIDBURN

—— One of Lancashire's best known inns is the Hark to Bounty in Slaidburn which was once known as just plain Dog. Then came the hunt which stopped for a glass or two before setting off in pursuit of a fox. The master, on hearing his favourite dog barking and howling in its desire to get on with the business of the day, was heard to remark 'Hark to Bounty' and the name stuck.

This is often the only entry relating to Slaidburn in guide books and even this may be folklore rather than fact; the inn, however, has one unique feature. One of the upstairs rooms served for many years as the courtroom for the Forest of Bowland. It took over this function when the old courthouse

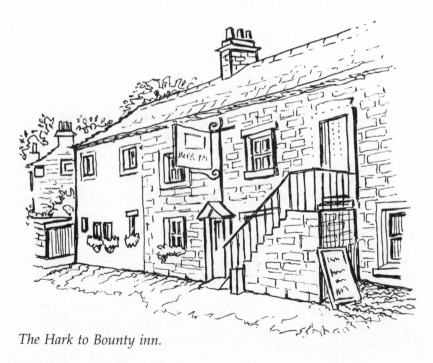

The Hark to Bounty inn.

was demolished. A window at the rear of the pub is studded with coloured glass and is thought to have been removed from the original building, the site of which is still remembered in the name of a field – Court House Close.

There is much more to the inn's courtroom than a mere name – it is still intact. It was provided with a separate doorway reached via a stone staircase close to the inn's entrance.

The inn serves excellent bar snacks and usually allows interested visitors to see the well-preserved courtroom. Within it is seating for spectators, the magistrates' bench and a very secure looking dock. All that it seems to lack is a prisoner but it is highly unlikely that you will be able to resist the temptation to stand in the dock yourself. Occasional functions are held in the courtroom at which time customers are literally 'called to the bar'.

STANDISH

—— Shops large and small line the streets of this large workaday village astride the busy A49 between Chorley and Wigan, combining to give the impression of Standish's origins as a small market town. Beyond the crossroads, the shops on one side give way to a wide square and the impressive stonework of St Wilfrid's church.

The church, with a market cross and stocks in front of it, dates mostly from the 16th century, except for its octagonal steeple which is an unfortunate example of Victorian meddling. Nevertheless, the church as a whole is extremely attractive, with a two-storey porch, buttressed tower and two domed turrets where the nave and chancel meet. The pulpit is Elizabethan. The monuments to local families are among the finest in Lancashire including the Wrightingtons, whose manor now forms part of a world famous orthopaedic hospital, the Chisnalls and especially the Standish clan. Miles Standish was the commander of a group of soldiers who went with the Pilgrim Fathers on the Mayflower to provide protection when they landed in the New World.

In the midst of all this history a reminder of the Civil War is always overlooked. This is a bullet spattered helmet worn by Edward Chisnall who fought for the king during the siege of

Lathom Hall of 1645. The Royalists were always under pressure here and their movements were very restricted. On the Parbold road is Cat-i'-th'-Window, a modern cottage with cats decorating a side wall and incorporating an older building. When placed in the window of this, a statue of a black cat informed Royalists, and later those who bravely adhered to the Catholic faith, that they could travel on in safety.

STANHILL

Stanhill is a small village which passes almost unnoticed but not quite absorbed by the urban sprawl connecting Oswaldtwistle and Blackburn. It is likely to become even more isolated following the construction of the M65 motorway link which caused so much local friction during the 1990s.

Look out for Stanhill post office and the plaque on the wall. It was in this building in 1745 that James Hargreaves was born; he later lived at nearby Rams Clough and some remnants of his cottage still remain in the hamlet.

Hargreaves invented the spinning jenny which revolution-ised the textile industry by making the spinning wheel redundant. The jenny could do the work of eight 'spinsters'. There are conflicting stories regarding the origin of the name jenny. The most often repeated is that in 1765 his daughter Jenny knocked over the spinning wheel and James noticed that the machine continued to rotate and that it would be possible to link eight wheels to one treddle in this position. Others say that it was Mrs Hargreaves who was called Jenny and that it was she who upset the wheel.

But probably James Hargreaves was more scientific than these theories suggest; he may have experimented over many years and it would be unlikely that he had such a sudden inspiration. The key surely is that Lancashire lads and lasses still often refer to any machine as a 'jinny' and this seems to pre-date Hargreaves' invention. The origin of the name, however, is just as much hidden as the hamlet of Stanhill where it all began.

From the 18th century onwards toll roads were built throughout Britain and specially designed houses were built from which the dues and demands could be collected. Lancashire, like other counties has lost many of these historical jigsaw pieces but some have remained.

One of the best preserved is at Steanor Bottom on the road from Todmorden to Rochdale via Littleborough. This toll house has been recently restored in splendid fashion with its toll board painted in bright letters.

Toll houses were obviously set at road junctions, with windows which allowed the keepers a good view of oncoming traffic. At the end of the Napoleonic Wars in 1815 there were plenty of ex-military men perfectly suited to guard the pikes and calculate the tolls. The gates were defended by pikes

Littleborough Coach House.

which could be turned to open them for traffic – hence turnpikes. Those who notice toll houses should not be confused by viewing them in a modern context. There were no side roads in those days – just a turnpike amid a morass of mud through which no wheeled traffic could pass. There was no alternative but to pay up!

Just beyond Steanor Bottom at Littleborough is the old coach house, entry to which is free. It holds regular exhibitions of work by local artists and photographers and the Grade II listed building also has a neat little café.

The coach house is sandwiched into a square made up by Holy Trinity church and the Falcon Inn and it was for the latter that the coach house was built. Littleborough was an important coaching stop between Lancashire and Yorkshire and by far the best inn of the period was the Falcon.

Opposite the Falcon Inn close to a set of traffic lights is another, unrestored, toll house, and whereas the Steanor toll house and the Littleborough coach house may not receive the attention they deserve from visitors, this relic of the past is completely ignored.

STOCKS

The village of Stocks is drowned beneath the waters of a reservoir which is now a bird watcher's paradise. It was constructed to supply water to the Fylde, achieved by damming the head waters of the river Hodder, a substantial tributary of the Ribble.

By the side of the reservoir at Dalehead is the tiny and deserted church of St James which is usually open and on its walls are newspaper cuttings describing the fate of Stocks village. Here were once around 20 cottages, a church, a shop, post office and a pub called the New Inn. It is possible to stand on the narrow road and look out over the water to a grassy island which during the breeding season echoes to the strident calls of a colony of black-headed gulls. The village lay to the right of the island and during periods of prolonged drought some of the collapsed walls of the buildings can occasionally be seen.

In 1925 the Fylde Water Board Act sealed the fate of the village and the demolition of the buildings began prior to the flooding of the Dalehead. As the church was being demolished on 12th November 1926 the Bishop of Bradford consecrated a new burial ground above the proposed water level; on the 30th July 1938 the new church of St James was consecrated, having been built using stone from the original church which itself only dated from 1852. Until then the villagers of Stocks had been obliged to travel to Slaidburn.

Standing watching the birds diving for food in the waters of the reservoir and with the occasional buzzard hovering overhead, it is hard not to say a prayer in memory of the dalesfolk of Stocks, who must have been devastated as they watched the water creep up to and then submerge their homes.

STYDD

——— Ribchester with its Roman museum, excellent pubs and splendid river scenery is among Lancashire's major tourist attractions. Situated close to the village is Stydd, a tiny and little visited collection of buildings. It is reached along a narrow farm-track leading off the road out of Ribchester towards Blackburn and close to a bridge over the Ribble.

Stydd has two remarkable buildings. On the left is a set of alms-houses built by the Shireburne family in 1726 and which have been kept in splendid repair ever since. They are still used for their original purpose of providing shelter for Roman Catholic ladies of the parish. There is a carefully preserved well in the garden and the entrance to the building is supported by four pillars which are said to have been brought from Ribchester Roman fort. These pillars have caused a great deal of controversy among historians specialising in ancient Lancashire. Some say they are not Roman and yet the four which support the porch of the White Bull in Ribchester are genuine. I have looked hard and long at both sets and am prepared to say that the Stydd set is indeed contemporary with that of the White Bull.

With regard to Stydd chapel there is less argument and here is one of the most interesting ecclesiastic buildings in Lanca-shire and yet it is usually deserted when Ribchester is bursting at the seams with visitors.

Stydd chapel is a fine example of Norman architecture and the building is all that remains of what was probably a substantial medieval infirmary run by the knights of St John of Jerusalem. The buildings of this order were dissolved during the 1530s on the orders of Henry VIII, then at loggerheads with the Pope over his proposed divorce from Catherine of Aragon.

A few years ago whilst making a television film about the river Ribble, I discovered that there was one aspect of the old hospice complex which was even unknown by those who had studied the building.

The Knights Hospitallers were skilled herbalists and it is still possible to explore their overgrown garden. Hereabouts grow comfrey, vervain, ground ivy, white deadnettle and many more medicinal herbs used in medieval England. It is perhaps this long tradition of healing the sick that gives one the feeling Stydd is a friendly place.

Inside the chapel there is little furniture but the basic structure has hardly been altered since its construction and the occasional service is still held within it. Otherwise this is barn owl and pipistrelle bat habitat but unlike many secluded churches is usually open during daylight hours. If closed the whereabouts of the key is usually indicated by a notice on the door.

SUNDERLAND

—— The wind often blasts across the mouth of the estuary of the river Lune, its entrance guarded by two of Morecambe Bay's most historic ports – Glasson Dock and Sunderland Point. These days Sunderland is quieter than its rival across the water because it is cut off twice each day by the tide which separates it from Overton.

The village of Sunderland is a fine example of an 18th century port and was the vision of a Quaker businessman, Robert Lawson. At that time the Lancaster area was fast developing trade links with North America and the West Indies and during this period sugar, rum, mahogany and slaves all flooded into Sunderland. It is suggested that the first cotton crop ever to enter Britain arrived here but lay idle for two years before anybody discovered what to do with it. We now know that Lancashire soon developed a use but in those early days it was wool and linen made from flax which were dominant and King Cotton was still lurking in the shadows.

There are still two tangible links with old-time Sunderland – the so-called cotton tree and Sambo's Grave. The 'cotton tree' seems to grow out of the base of an old warehouse recently converted into pleasant cottages. This probably arrived by accident rather than being deliberately planted. It is actually a Kapok tree (*Bombax pentandrum*) which is native to the West Indies. Although now over 200 years old and showing some signs of age the tree still manages to produce some blossom each year. The 'cotton tree' is not signed but is easy to find.

Sambo's grave, on the other hand, is signed but many visitors give up before they reach the remote spot. The route follows a pretty hedgerow and emerges onto the seashore which is overlooked, but thankfully and perhaps surprisingly not dominated, by Heysham Nuclear Power Station.

In 1736 a black slave was landed here and his master, of whom he had grown fond, went off on business and Sambo is alleged to have died of grief. Probably the poor chap died of 'flu or another complaint brought on by an unfamiliar climate. Whatever the cause of his demise he is buried in unconsecrated ground facing the wind and the waves. A later clergyman relented and a commemorative verse was placed over the grave. This is still there (although the words have been re-inscribed) and the local children keep the grave well supplied with wild flowers. The verse reads:

> Full many a Sand-bird chirps upon the Sod
> And many a moonlight Elfin round him trips
> Full many a Summer's Sunbeam warms the Clod
> And many a teeming cloud upon him drips.
> But still he sleeps – till the awakening Sounds
> Of the Archangel's Trump now life impart
> Then the GREAT JUDGE his approbation founds
> Not on man's COLOR but his worth of heart.

Personally I would rather be hidden away in this lovely spot than hemmed in by the marble monstrosities of a modern day cemetery. In response to those who ask if a spirit can be happy in unconsecrated ground I feel inclined to answer – God knows!

TARLETON

Situated on the old Preston to Liverpool road, and close to the estuary of the Ribble is the ancient village of Tarleton, now bypassed by a new road.

Nearby and still on the busy 'new' road is Tarleton's 'old' church, which is one of the finest buildings in the north-west. St Mary's dates to 1719 and is brick built apart from the belfry tower which is of beautifully cut stone. Since it was replaced by a larger church in 1886 the old building, constructed by the lord of the manor, is redundant. There is a notice by the porch, however, which explains that it is still maintained by the Redundant Churches Fund administered from the unusually named St Andrew's-by-the-Wardrobe church on Queen Victoria Street, London.

The cemetery of St Mary's is still used, and maintained wonderfully well, but the church itself is sensibly kept locked. It is possible, however, to see through the window to where the old oil lamps remain, as does the splendid Georgian gallery reached via a staircase.

The overall feeling you get of this church is that despite the proximity of a modern road, tranquillity is still easily found by those who are prepared to park their car in the old village and cross the busy road to its now isolated church.

TOCKHOLES

Whenever Lancashire's forgotten villages are discussed the first on the list is always Wycoller, perhaps proving that this place is not actually forgotten! Way down on the list comes Tockholes, which should be pronouced to rhyme with cockles. It lies about three miles to the south of Blackburn and is tucked into a fold on Darwen Moor. The only mention that this triangular shaped village usually warrants these days is during the early snows of winter which block the narrow winding roads leading out of the settlement. Tockholes is the first village to be cut off and the last to attract visitors.

The village has a long and fascinating history and is thought to derive its name from Toka's Hol. There was possibly a 9th-century chieftain named Tok who settled in this hollow. The search for its ancient history should begin in the churchyard where an alternative derivation of the name is suggested. A stone 'cross' bears the inscription 'The upper portion of this monument is supposed to be a remnant of the old parish preaching cross, possibly dating back to AD 684. The lower portion is probably part of the ancient Toches stone from which the parish takes its name.'

'Serious' historians point out that there are too many possibilities and not enough certainties; the fact remains, however, that there was an ancient church on this site, even though the present St Stephen's is relatively recent. A Saxon church was here in AD 640 but had been replaced by 1494. The present church is 19th-century. There was a time when the church specialised in open air services, especially in the 19th and early 20th centuries, a stone pulpit built in 1910 near the church is a reminder of this time. Almost hidden among a tangle of churchyard vegetation is a monument which is a sad reminder of a man who nearly became rich. Some inventors of textile machinery either made a fortune, a reputation or both. John Osbaldeston (1780-1862) deserved both but got neither. His inscription reads:

Here lies
John Osbaldeston
A humble inventor
Who raised many to wealth and fortune
But himself lived in poverty and died in obscurity
The dupe of false friends
And the
Victim of misplaced confidence.

John's main contribution to the textile industry was the invention of the weft-fork, a simple but very important device which stopped a power loom whenever the weft snapped. This saved the cotton manufacturers a great deal of money but the device was so easy to copy that John was paid nothing. He died in Blackburn workhouse and had it not been for the kindly vicar of Tockholes this 'man of cotton' would have been tossed into a pauper's grave.

John Osbaldeston may have been deprived of fame in life but his name should never be forgotten.

Turton Tower.

🌿 TURTON

——— There are two suggested derivations of the word Turton. It may have Scandinavian religious connections and mean 'Thors Town' whilst other historians think it could mean 'Tower Town'.

People who have never been to Lancashire still think of the county only as a land of mill chimneys and smoke. This was not right even in the 1890s and it is far from the truth a century later. No Lancashire town is more than a mile or two from open hills which are full of wildlife. Here is the home of the short-eared owl which can often be seen hunting across the open spaces. This is one of the owls which usually hunts by day. The moors around Turton are full of short-tailed field voles on which the short-eared owls feed.

There is a stone circle on Turton Moor which was of great importance in Neolithic and Bronze Age times. But this site is totally ignored, even by scholars, who disagree generally on the significance of stone circles. It is suggested that they may have been temples or massive astronomical calendars; but it is certain that even smaller circles were important for many centuries. Turton Tower is also neglected but is an historical gem and its gardens are a haven for wildlife. The present house is constructed around a pele tower covered in red Virginia creeper and built about 1400. At this time it provided a defence for the Torboc family not just against the invading Scots but also against their own relatives with whom they were always feuding.

The impressive half-timbering was added by the Orrel family who followed the Torbocs but in 1628 they fell on hard times and sold it to Humphrey Chetham, who allowed the Orrels to remain in residence. This is surprising as during the Civil War of the 1640s the Orrels supported the king but Chetham was firmly behind Cromwell. Humphrey Chetham is remembered in the name of the pub in nearby Chapeltown, and also as the founder of the famous school in the centre of Manchester.

After Chetham, Turton was sold to the Greenes, the Freres and in 1835 to the Kayes. This family followed the Victorian tradition and built follies and extravagant extensions, but the main building retained its character.

Turton Tower is now a fascinating museum well organised by Lancashire County Council. This reflects the history of the building and there is also a small tea-room and shop. It is the Bronze Age circle, however, reached via a footpath up onto the moors which is the forgotten monument of the county.

UP HOLLAND

—— Visitors flock to Lancaster Priory which is a much altered church influenced by monastic architecture and also to Whalley Abbey which is a majestic ruin. Up Holland, however, is usually ignored and yet here not far from Wigan, the oldest borough in Lancashire, is a priory, substantial parts of which would still be recognised by the monks who built it.

The priory was founded in 1307 on the orders of Bishop of Lichfield in Staffordshire. This bishop was responsible for all of present day Lancashire south of the Ribble until 1541 when the diocese of Chester was established.

Although the chancel at Up Holland only dates to 1882 the magnificent nave was actually the monks' choir. The tower is a strange structure as it seems to be dwarfed by the church rather than the other way round. Scholars, however, have looked carefully at the late 15th-century plans and discovered that the tower was meant to be much higher. Whether the monks ran out of money is not confirmed but what was actually constructed does give the priory church a rather out of scale appearance.

What does remain is still impressive and it is hard to believe that Up Holland Priory is not high on the list of Lancashire's tourist attractions.

It is fortunate that the priory church has survived as a memorial to a family who were far from fortunate. The funds to construct the buildings were provided by Robert de Holland who later betrayed John of Gaunt, the Earl of Lancaster and was beheaded in consequence.

By the mid 15th century the family fortunes had not recovered and the last of the founders of Up Holland was very much down on his luck. After a period of begging in Flanders he was found drowned, probably not accidentally, just off the Kent coast at Dover.

VULCAN

——— This long forgotten village close to Newton on Merseyside is not a reminder of Mr Spock of the Star Ship Enterprise, but a wonderful memory of the days of steam. It was built in 1840 as a base for the construction of steam locomotives for the Liverpool and Manchester Railway Company. Surprisingly attractive cottages were built around a spacious village green and were the homes for the workers of the Vulcan Iron Foundry.

Close to the parish church of St Peter is a memorial to Peers Naylor which carries the humorous rhyme

'My Engine now is cold and still,
No water does my boiler fill
My Coke affords its flame no more,
My days of usefulness are o'er.'

Between Newton and St Helens is Earlstown. Here George and Robert Stephenson's Sankey viaduct was constructed to cross the St Helens Canal and was the first such structure in the world to carry passengers.

WADDINGTON

I'll sing you a song of a streamlet so clear
A gem of the moorland renowned far and near:
The bold sons of Bolland dark legends of tell
Of the moss-mantled banks of Walloper Well
CHORUS
Walloper Well on Waddington Fell
'Mid bloom of the heather and bonny bluebell:
These lovers oft tell, each beau to his belle
The olden time story of Walloper Well.

The mason who built it, in love with the maid,
Who brought him his dinner, one day it is said,
Was struggling to kiss her, when over the Fell
A Pedlar then passing cried 'Wallop her Well'.

The cheeks of the maiden were reddened with shame
Her lover, with laughter adopted the name;
And so through the pedlar who came o'er the Fell
He christened the fountain 'Walloper Well'.

Despite this imaginative, if somewhat sexist, poem it is more likely that the name derives from the Old English word meaning a spring. By far the best way to approach Waddington is along the fell road, with the bubbling sound of a courting curlew in your ears and the heavy scent of nectar-full heather hanging in the air. Just beyond the Moorcock Inn the road dips steeply into the village which is sliced in two by a stream dancing to the tune made by water chattering over the smooth pebbles on the bed.

On one side of the stream is Waddington Hall, privately owned but easily seen from the main road, whilst the other is dominated by the magnificently proportioned tower of the parish church dedicated to St Helen. This lady was reputed to be a British, princess and the mother of Constantine the Great, who was born at York and embraced the Christian religion on behalf of the Roman Empire. Surely this was the most important conversion in the history of Christianity with the possible exception of St Paul. The oldest part of the present church is the tower which is almost certainly 16th century, but one of the stained glass windows is of particular interest since it traces the history of Waddington village, including a portrait of the Saxon Wada from whom the village derives its name. He was, apparently, a real tough guy who was leader of the local tribe around AD 798, and he is shown with a fearsome assemblage of weapons and in full war-paint. This fascinating window is completed by a portrait of St Helen, and another of Henry VI with his crown in his hand, preparing to hand it over to his victors.

It is very appropriate that this poor Lancastrian king should be commemorated in Waddington, which must have had such painful memories for him. After a reign of 35 years Henry VI was certainly weak in body and also in mind (he had fits of insanity), which did not give him much of a chance of hanging on to his crown even though he had a number of loyal subjects. Following a heavy defeat at Hexham in 1464 Henry fled and eventually arrived at the home of the Pudsays at Bolton-by-Bowland where he was given shelter for almost a year. He then moved on to Waddington Hall, one of the homes of the Lancastrian supporter Sir John Tempest. Thomas Talbot, his son-in-law, was a Yorkist and the king's where-abouts was soon known. Once more on the run he was captured at the stepping stones at Brungerley, near Clitheroe (see also *Brungerley*).

For their share in giving up the Lancastrian monarch to the Yorkists the Talbots received a reward from Edward IV. In addition to all their costs and charges, Sir Thomas Talbot was given the sum of £100 and a yearly pension of £40. The hall was later used as a farm house but the splendid building was saved and one of Britain's most historic sites tucked quietly away off the main street has a secure future.

The village has several inns, including the Lower and Higher Buck, a sign that deer were once hunted here when thick woodland lay in the valley and probably upon Waddington Fell also. This may partly account for the gift of Robert Parker of Browsholme Hall, who was in charge of the local hunting grounds. On the left of the road beyond the Higher Buck, on the way to West Bradford, a tablet over a gate records the building of alms-houses by Robert Parker in 1701. Through the gate all of the old buildings remain, constructed around a lovely green and sheltered by fine old beech trees. The ancient water pump is still there as is the chapel which once meant that the little community was self-sufficient. It is still a pretty and secret place even today and Robert Parker had anticipated the old age pension by around 200 years!

WADDOW

—— Waddow Hall, situated between Clitheroe and Waddington, is a Tudor building constructed as a dower house for the Tempest family and it was used by them until 1657. It then passed by marriage into the Starkie family who made so many alterations that even historians sometimes fail to date it correctly.

Since 1927 Waddow has been owned by the Girl Guides' Association which sometimes leads people to assume that it is impossible to see despite the fact that a public footpath runs close to it.

Apart from lots of good girls Waddow is also famous for one particularly bad girl known as Peg O'Well (or Peg O' Nell). Apparently Peg was a serving wench who frequently got the wrong side of Mistress Starkie. The lady got so cross with the wilful lass that on a cold frosty morning she sent her out to the well and shouted after her that she hoped she would fall and break her neck. This is just what the unfortunate girl did and the remorseful Mistress Starkie erected a statue to the servant close to the well where she died.

In the superstitious days of the time, sacrifices of cats and poultry were made by local folk who believed the legend that Peg claimed a life lost by drowning in the nearby river Ribble at least once every year. As soon as a reliable bridge crossed the river and replaced the stepping-stones death by drowning at times of flood became a thing of the past.

The fear has still not quite gone and Peg's statue down by the old well shows signs of wear and tear. She did not lose her head because of erosive effects of time, however, but because somebody got their own back on the evil spirit and smote it off with an axe!

Allen Clarke's book *Windmill Land* describes the Fylde in the days just before and during the 1914-18 war. A keen cyclist, he described his journey to Warton which he said had 'an old peg mill which you can see from the main road. The mill lane runs down to the Guides' House, an inn and the bank of the Ribble a mile away'.

On his way he describes passing a 'big aerodrome' where the first great aviation display ever held in the British Isles took place in 1909. This is now Blackpool Airport.

How could this explorer on a bike have realised that the tiny village of Warton would also have an airfield and eventually produce some of the world's greatest military aircraft?

What is left of the scene which Allen Clarke described? British Aerospace have spread out so far that it is not possible to follow Mill Lane right down to the river, but this can be approached via East Naze Lane in Freckleton. The left turn to the Industrial Estate should be ignored and further on the road veers left alongside the airstrip and ends at a layby close to a muddy lane.

The temptation to drive down this lane should be resisted because the walk is splendid and leads to the site of the Bush Inn. Alas this has been demolished and so has the Guides' House which once stood near the fording point across the river Ribble and its tributary the Douglas feeding in on the opposite bank. In the days before the modern airfield was built both the Bush and the Guides' House served ham and eggs and there was a circular walk from Warton church down to the river. These days the only human visitors are bird and aeroplane spotters.

Nature has now taken over the area once occupied by the old inn and growing in profusion is ragwort, campion and teasel. The sharp seed heads of this plant were once used to raise the nap on cloth and they are still used by some companies who make the cloth for snooker tables.

In Mill Lane is a scrap yard belonging to E. H. Mapple and Son. Among the pile of old Austins, MGs, racing cars and battered caravans is the oak post of the mill, some of the huge mill stones and one of the large tiles taken from the room where the grain was dried. This has small perforations in it through which hot air was pumped by bellows.

Of all the mills on the Fylde Warton's was the most unique. The whole mill turned around a wooden centre post. It is thought that the mill was built in Lincolnshire, then transferred to Rufford on the Southport side of the Ribble. Around 1770 it was taken to pieces and moved across the river to Warton. The mill last ground corn around 1914 but was pretty well derelict at this time despite some money being given for its preservation by Sir Joseph Beecham, the owner of Beecham's Pills and father of Sir Thomas Beecham the famous orchestral conductor.

Mr Mapple revealed that he has no intention of letting the remaining peg and millstones disappear. Perhaps, 80 years on, another grant will be forthcoming to help preserve these famous relics.

WARTON

Situated near Carnforth and just off the A6 is another Warton, an ancient village with its church dedicated to St Oswald. Oswald was the second Christian king of Northumbria, who became a convert on the island of Iona. In AD 650 he was murdered by the heathen King Penda of Mercia.

On the top of the hill on Main Street and opposite the post office is Washington House which was rebuilt during the 18th century and is now privately owned. Visitors from the United States find the house fascinating, but it is to the church that they flock. Robert Washington, who died in 1483, paid for the tower to be constructed. Originally, the Washington coat-of-arms showed three mullets and two bars, these later became adapted to form the famous stars and stripes.

Competing with the church as Warton's most historic treasure but usually ignored is the ruined Old Rectory, now maintained by English Heritage. Because of the importance of the church the rectory's claim to fame is seldom realised despite it being a unique survival of the architecture of the period. This building was constructed during the 14th century when the Scots were invading the north-west. The rectory with its thick castle-like walls was built by the de Thweng family who usually appointed its own members as rectors of the church. The building was also used as the court of justice.

Once the rectory had ceased to administer justice the court moved to the Shovel Inn (then called the Malt-Shovel) which

The ruins of Warton rectory.

functioned as a cross between a magistrates' court and a solicitor's office. The Shovel was also an important stop on the coach route to Kendal which passed through the village until 1792.

The history of the other family which dominated the area is less well known but is likely to come into the spotlight in the future. The Kitsons of Warton Hall had a daughter Margaret, who married John Washington, and her brother Thomas, born here in 1485, moved to Hengrave in Sussex. Here his daughter Katherine was born; she married John Spencer Churchill. Fancy that – George Washington and Winston Churchill were actually related. Also descended from this line is Lady Diana Spencer who married Prince Charles. Warton's history may well eventually also lay claim to being part of the roots of a reigning monarch.

WHALLEY

The name Whalley is said to be Saxon and meaning the 'place of the wells'. Having good supplies of fresh water it was in an ideal place for the establishment of an important settlement. Some historians claim that St Augustine founded a church here as early as the 7th century. A white wooden church was built and ruled over by deans and until very recent times the parish of Whalley was the largest in

Lancashire. The village stands astride the Lancashire Calder which then flows on for a mile or so to its union with the river Ribble. With its attractive huddle of old coaching inns, tea shops, antique and up-market dress shops, Whalley is a tourist's delight.

Whalley has become particularly attractive since the A59 bypass was constructed and visitors can enjoy a quiet walk around the extensive ruins of the 14th-century Cistercian abbey and the even older parish church which is one of the finest in Lancashire. Most, however, miss the magnificent churchyard crosses which are even older. Here are three different styles of cross within a few feet of each other – Anglo Celtic, Anglian and Anglo-Norse.

One of the crosses is said to be contemporary with St Augustine although not all historians agree but the latest date for any of them is the early 10th century. The tallest of the crosses is certainly the oldest although all three blend in with the forest-like mass of other mainly Victorian memorials. In this sense the Whalley crosses are indeed hidden but it is lucky indeed that they were not lost altogether.

During the Commonwealth period of the 1650s every semblance of papist idolatry was supposed to be removed and the crosses were hacked off their bases and thrown into the ditch which until its dissolution had served as the leet for the abbey corn mill. There the crosses lay out of sight and out of mind until restored to their bases by a vicar in the 18th century and where they have stood ever since.

*   *   *

Until a bridge was built near the confluence of the rivers Calder and Ribble near Whalley the row ferry known as Hacking Boat was set on a busy meeting point. Nearby Hacking Hall was then known to all Lancashire's travellers, now it is a private farmhouse set in splendid isolation but its exterior delights can easily be seen snuggling close to the old ferry point which is on a quiet footpath. The hall is not very well known these days, the Saxon barn being passed without notice and yet it may well be one of the oldest buildings in the whole of Lancashire.

Hacking Hall was the original manor of the Hackyng family until it passed by marriage into the hands of the Shuttleworths in 1336. In 1258 William of Hackyng had given some lands to the monks of Stanlaw abbey to build a barn and this still exists today. The abbey was originally on the Wirral bank of the Mersey, but it was subject to flooding and later moved its site to nearby Whalley on the river Calder.

A local pub called the Judge Walmesly celebrates the fact that this legal gentleman needed all of his skills as an advocate to absorb his estate with that of Hacking, then owned by his wife Anne Shuttleworth. Legal battles were long and furious from 1568 until almost the end of the century. In 1607 the judge rebuilt Hacking Hall which is a fine example of Jacobean architecture.

 ## WHEATLEY LANE

———— In Wheatley Lane, now a quiet hamlet just off the Padiham to Barrowford bypass, is a chapel which was once of great importance to the 18th century Inghamite sect.

Everyone has heard of John Wesley and his chapels are found throughout the world. A great friend of the Wesleys was Benjamin Ingham and for a while in the mid-18th century it seemed that the Inghamite sect would also become a major influence on ecclesiatical evolution.

Benjamin Ingham was born at Ossett in Yorkshire in 1712 and seems to have been a much milder character than John Wesley. A good scholar, Benjamin left Batley grammar school and went to Oxford where he soon became embroiled in religious politics. He was ordained with the Wesleys and accompanied John and Charles to Georgia.

On his return to England, in 1741 John Ingham met and married the youngest daughter of the Earl of Huntingdon. He worked closely with the Moravian sect but after breaking with them in 1754 his supporters named themselves Inghamites. Gradually, however, the followers of Ingham decreased in numbers and few of their chapels remain. Hardly anyone, except the faithful few, visit the Wheatley Lane chapel with its quaint little cemetery and the only feature noted by those who pass through Wheatley Lane is the monkey puzzle tree in front of the chapel, completed in 1750. The sect once had an influential following and it is well worth while searching out an 18th-century inscription on the outer wall of the chapel which reads

'Sacred to the Memory of James Cowgill, surgeon and apothecary of Priestfield near Colne. His usefulness in administrating medicine will be long remembered. He died in the exercise of repentance towards God and and faith in our Lord Jesus Christ'.

WIGAN

—— This surprisingly attractive town is smothered by a smoke-screen of music hall jokes and innuendos regarding the cloth capped image of the most famous Rugby League team in the world. It will certainly survive even the 1995 decision of the Union authority to admit publicly that they are professional.

Wigan Pier is not just part of the title of George Orwell's book but a masterpiece of a museum in its own right and nearby Haigh Hall is a country park which also has its supply of visitors.

Wigan, however, is the oldest borough in Lancashire and the Romans had an important crossroads on the site. It was called Coccium. The 'Wigan station' was a 'branch line' on Watling Street which linked Warrington and Ribchester. A Roman altar can be seen by those with keen eyesight, situated close to a window ledge in the parish church and incorporated into the stonework.

Near the Roman altar is the tomb of Sir William Bradshaw of Haigh Hall and his wife Mabel. It is this lady who warrants a substantial entry in Wigan's less-known history. Sir William is shown in heraldic posture, his hand resting close to his sword and obviously ready for action. He was a formidable battler but at this point history and folklore become confused. He went off to fight for king and country either during the crusades or the battle of Bannockburn. It took him a long time to find his way home and after ten years Lady Mabel assumed him dead and married a 'Welsh Knight'. Welsh in those days meant any foreigner or 'one coming from afar'.

Sir William was obviously not a good timekeeper and turned up immediately following his wife's nuptials. For some reason he was dressed as a beggar but this did not prevent him from buckling on his sword, attacking and killing the 'Welsh' knight.

Lady Mabel was obviously not too happy either and was determined to do penance for her bigamous act. Once a week she made the journey from Haigh Hall to Wigan church on her knees and carrying a burning taper. Her journey ended not within the church but at a preaching cross now situated on the main road near a school.

This has been known ever since as Mab's Cross and Sir Walter Scott used the events, but adding his usual touch of poetic licence in his novel *The Betrothed*.

WINTER HILL

—— One of Lancashire's high spots is Winter Hill standing 1,437 feet above Bolton and now dominated by an ITA television transmitter mast, itself higher than 1,000 feet. There is also a small control building beneath the mast.

For centuries the hill has been the haunt of curlew, skylark, pipit and the occasional golden plover. In recent years hen harriers have also been recorded.

Since 1838 an iron pillar has shared the boggy moorland with the clumps of reed. The pillar bears the inscription 'In memory of George Henderson, Traveller, a Native of Annan, Dumfrieshire, who was barbarously murdered on Rivington Moor at Noonday November 9th 1838 in the 20th year of his age'.

George was on his way with his pack of merchandise from Horwich to the Black Dog inn at Belmont where he had arranged to meet a friend. When young Henderson failed to turn up his friend set off into the mist to search. He found him dying of a gunshot wound to the head and all he was able to say was that he had been robbed.

The Scotsman's friend had passed a tall man with a gun whom he was later able to identify as a local collier by the name of Whittle. He was, however, acquitted at Lancaster assizes through lack of evidence.

George Henderson was buried at Blackburn which was the base from which he worked and for a number of years on the anniversary of his death a Scots piper played a haunting lament high up on Winter Hill. How pleasant it would be to see this tradition restored, for the sounds of almost forgotten history are obviously even rarer than the sights.

WISWELL

Snuggled into the foothills of Pendle Hill not far from Whalley is the tiny, historic but little known hamlet of Wiswell, locally pronounced as Wisel.

Known until very recently as the damson blossom village Wiswell was the birthplace of John Paslew the last and ill-fated abbot of Whalley. Wiswell Farm has been constructed on the site of the Paslew family dwelling but incorporated into its structure are several substantial chunks, including mullioned windows, taken from Old Wiswell Hall.

In 1536 John Paslew involved his abbey in the Pilgrimage of Grace. This was brought about by the suppression of the smaller monasteries and also because of the fears of Catholics who quite rightly saw the Reformation as a threat to the power of the Pope.

A window from Abbot Paslew's birthplace, now incorporated into the newer dwelling.

Henry VIII cracked down hard mainly on those concentrated in the northern counties, who had initiated this resistance to his will and Abbot Paslew was tried at Lancaster. He was convicted of high treason on 10th March 1537 and hanged two days later having been abbot of Whalley for 30 years.

Wiswell has retained all its old world charm, although building has to some extent kept up with the times. There are two features, both almost smothered by a tangle of vegetation which a reincarnated abbot would easily recognise. These are the old preaching cross and the well from which the village takes its name. The cross served as a preaching station and also as a sacred place to rest coffins being carried for burial at Whalley church. The old well is difficult to find but is situated off the main street and a short distance along Moor Lane on the left.

Once the well has been found most of Wiswell's secrets have been uncovered – we have an abbot, a cross and a well. But who was Wis who owned the well?

WOODPLUMPTON

The Lancashire Witches of 1612 have become so famous that all other tales of the supernatural in the county tend to be overshadowed. Here is one such lesser-known account.

A small village on the outskirts of Preston on the old road to Blackpool, Woodplumpton is said to mean 'an enclosure near a plum tree on the edge of a forest'. The present church, dedicated to St Anne, looks modern as it was substantially rebuilt in 1900. Christian worship, however, has been celebrated on the site at least since the 11th century and probably long before. Such a sacred site is hardly the place to go witch-hunting but here lies Meg, a far from merry lass who caused chaos in the area.

Marjorie Hilton, the Fylde witch, was born at Catforth and eventually met her death by being crushed between a wall and a runaway barrel, much to the joy of the local population which was terrified of her.

This may have been because she was by that time old, ugly and bad-tempered with her actions taking on a greater significance as late 17th-century folk were much more gullible and superstitious than we are today.

When she died it was discovered that Mad Bad Meg had been born a Christian and as she had never been 'examined as a witch' she had the right to be buried in St Anne's churchyard. A compromise was reached and Meg was duly buried during the night of 2nd May 1705 with only the light of torches to guide the bearers. Apparently this did not please Meg and she is said to have scratched her way out of her grave and caused more trouble when dead than she had when alive. She was reburied but again refused to rest in peace and was interred for a third time. This time the villagers took no chances and she was buried head first and her grave was covered by a huge boulder which presses down on her remains to the present day.

Some feel, however that Meg still has the last word and base their belief upon two pieces of evidence. A young boy visiting the church with his parents and not knowing the story of the Fylde witch went into the church ahead of the adults. He emerged terrified and insisted that he had been chased out by an angry wizened woman dressed in 'old clothes'. In the 1940s a very level-headed farmer by the name of Major Wingard asserted that he had seen the ghost of Meg Shelton. This is one Lancashire spirit which apparently refuses to be suppressed despite the huge boulder pinning her down.

WORSLEY

——— Now hemmed in by the M62 and a myriad of feeder roads and roundabouts Worsley has become popular with tourists because here begins the story of the Bridgewater canal, the first to be constructed and be independent of a river. Most visitors content themselves with a stroll along the banks of the canal but they ignore three remarkable features all within walking distance.

One mile to the north is Wardley Hall, the residence of the bishops of Salford. This 16th-century building is known as the Skull House because within is the skull of a Benedictine monk named Ambrose Barlow who fell foul of the religious persecution of the 16th century.

On the opposite side of the road complex splitting the main village is Worsley Old Hall, the home of the Duke of Bridgewater. Its main buildings were constructed during the 19th century but around a central Tudor core. When the Bridge-water canal was being constructed its builder James Brindley lived at the Old Hall. When the canal was opened on 17th July 1761 there was much more of it hidden than could be seen. The cut seems to emerge from a steep cliff of red sandstone, but within, some 46 miles of underground tunnels lead to the coal faces. These tunnels were not simple cuts but working canals with inclined planes and locks.

The water is red with rust oozing from the iron in the rocks of the old workings but a careful look will reveal the sunken wrecks of the boats which once brought out the coal into the main canal. These boats were kept simple to reduce costs and their timbers stuck out like ribs. They were therefore called Starvation Boats.

WORSTON

The object of most village greens was to provide a focus for social events. This must have happened at Worston but the part of the modern village facing the world has altered, leaving the old green hidden at the rear of the Calfs Head inn which now has a fine reputation for food and accommodation.

In the summer you may need to scramble about among bracken, bramble and willowherb so a winter visit may be the best idea if you wish to find the bull ring embedded in the grass.

Bull baiting was a popular 'sport' in the middle ages, the unfortunate animal being tied to the ring and then the bull-terriers set upon it. What could be regarded as a waste of valuable protein was excused by the assertion that the baiting tenderised the flesh of the bull, which was then eagerly sought by the gourmets of the period.

WORTHINGTON LAKES

Worthington Lakes are situated between Chorley and Wigan near Standish and just off the A49 which was one of the earliest turnpike roads in Lancashire. Keep a sharp look out and you will find some of the original iron mile-markers still in position. These were made at the Haigh Iron Foundry at Wigan in 1837.

Those approaching from Chorley will pass the White Crow inn on the left. The approach from the opposite direction is via another hostelry, the Boar's Head dating to the 16th century and once a vitally important coaching inn.

At Worthington there is an extensive car park, lots of picnic tables, an information centre, café and a classroom which schools can hire for the day.

From the information centre a well-marked route follows the shoreline of three reservoirs and around the edge of a conservation area before swinging around and following the opposite bank. After crossing several fields head to the right and pass under the water tower and return to the car park.

The three reservoirs here are fed by two substantial streams, but an even larger river actually flows beneath the lakes. During the construction of Worthington, Arley and Adlington reservoirs in the late 19th century, the river Douglas was actually culverted and now flows beneath them. The Douglas is therefore Lancashire's hidden river. Adlington provides water for a bleach works whilst Worthington and Arley provide drinking water for the Wigan area. There is a water treatment works at the lower end and this can filter and chlorinate up to four million gallons per day after which it is pumped to a covered storage reservoir which is only 1½ miles away.

Since 1977 Worthington has functioned as a small country park and fishing is allowed. Anglers catch trout, barbel, rudd, roach and perch. At Arley there are barbel, carp, tench, bream and roach; whilst Adlington has carp, bream, tench, roach, perch and gudgeon.

Those who feel that an area sandwiched between Wigan and Chorley cannot be either pretty or of interest to naturalists should not be misled for here is a nature reserve to rival any set much deeper in open countryside. Roe deer wander around the wooded areas fringing the reservoirs and other common mammals include rabbit, grey squirrel, long-tailed field mouse, bank vole and both stoat and weasel.

Worthington Lakes would provide a delightful and gentle walk for the scenery alone but the fact that important ornithological research is going on is a bonus, as is the fact that beneath it is an underground river!

WYCOLLER HALL

Once described as Lancashire's lost village, Wycoller has been brought back to life in recent years by becoming the focus for a country park. It also lies on the Brontë Way, a footpath of around ten miles linking Haworth and Colne.

Charlotte Brontë knew Wycoller well with its three ancient bridges, a clapper, a clam and a packhorse, crossing the beck. She used the now ruined hall as the blueprint for Ferndean Manor in *Jane Eyre* which was published in 1847. Ferndean was where Rochester, blinded in a fire at Thornfield Hall started by and which killed his wife, at last found solace with Jane the governess he loved.

The now ruined and almost forgotten hall was built in Tudor times and has a ghostly tale to tell. This was not used by Charlotte Brontë but I wonder what impression it made on Emily whose *Wuthering Heights* is actually one of the best tales of the supernatural ever written.

Once a year on a wild windy night, a ghostly horseman is said to gallop up to the hall, charge into the building and up the stairs which have long since collapsed along with all the upper rooms. A woman's screams echo through the night and the horseman retraces his evil route before disappearing into the night.

One legend tells us that one of the Cunliffe family who owned the hall in the 17th century, killed his wife at Wycoller Hall whilst another version suggests that a fox being hunted by a male Cunliffe sought refuge in my lady's chamber and was ripped apart in front of her by the hounds.

Either could be true because the Cunliffes were a blood-thirsty lot. There is documentary evidence that in 1819 the last male squire died without issue and breathed his last into a pillow stained by the blood of two fighting cocks brought into his bedroom to entertain him.

INDEX